# Mini MARVELS

*15 Little Quilts with Big Style*

*Compiled by Lissa Alexander*

Martingale®
*Create with Confidence*

## Dedication

This book is dedicated to everyone who loves cutting up fabric and stitching it back together—to create, to make, to express!

It is also dedicated to Lissa Alexander. It's been written that, "Life is about the people you meet and the things you create with them." Lissa creates magic. She sees the best in people, their potential to do extraordinary things.

The 16 ladies whose work is shown here have two things in common: we love to stitch and we love Lissa. With words of encouragement and wisdom, a nurturing heart and a shoulder to lean on, she has helped us live our dreams!

Moda All-Stars
Mini Marvels: 15 Little Quilts with Big Style
© 2016 by Martingale & Company®

Martingale®
19021 120th Ave. NE, Ste. 102
Bothell, WA 98011-9511 USA
ShopMartingale.com

Printed in China
21 20 19 18 17 16          8 7 6 5 4 3 2 1

Library of Congress Cataloging-in-Publication Data is available upon request.

ISBN: 978-1-60468-842-9

## MISSION STATEMENT

We empower makers who use fabric and yarn to make life more enjoyable.

## CREDITS

**PUBLISHER AND CHIEF VISIONARY OFFICER**
Jennifer Erbe Keltner

**CONTENT DIRECTOR**
Karen Costello Soltys

**MANAGING EDITOR**
Tina Cook

**ACQUISITIONS EDITOR**
Karen M. Burns

**TECHNICAL EDITOR**
Ellen Pahl

**COPY EDITOR**
Sheila Chapman Ryan

**DESIGN MANAGER**
Adrienne Smitke

**PRODUCTION MANAGER**
Regina Girard

**COVER AND INTERIOR DESIGNER**
Connor Chin

**PHOTOGRAPHER**
Brent Kane

**ILLUSTRATOR**
Christine Erikson

# Contents

# Introduction

*Small and mighty. A little something extra. Everything small is a big deal these days. And why not? If full sized is cute, smaller is even cuter. In the pages that follow, you'll find patterns by 15 Moda All-Star designers. They may be little quilts, but you'll love their look in a big way!*

*A mini-quilt is a marvel you can start and finish in a flash! You can have it done and on display right away. It's almost-instant gratification. Make your own gallery wall of mini marvels to showcase all your favorite Moda fabrics. It's the perfect way to experiment with new-to-you techniques, color palettes, and styles—and to showcase in a big way how much you love to quilt!*

*Besides having the best collection of mini patterns in one marvelous book, you'll also find out for the first time ever what the sewing superpowers are of your favorite designers. The secrets are out! Enjoy learning the inside scoop.*

*Whether you've made lots of mini-quilts or this is your first foray into something small, I hope you love what's inside. And know that your little-quilt book purchase is making a big difference. Royalties are being donated to Texas Scottish Rite Hospital for Children, a leader in the treatment of pediatric orthopedic conditions. The work these people do is miraculous and the patients are **mini marvels.** So big thanks to you! We think quilters are marvel-ous!*

*~Lissa Alexander*

# Bright Sun

*Choose a cheerful variety of prints from your scrap basket or from a Layer Cake to make a sweet and simple mini-quilt that will add some sunshine to any room, no matter the season.*

Designed by Sherri McConnell;
machine quilted by Abby Latimer

**Finished size:** 15" x 19"
**Finished block:** 4" x 4"

## Materials

*Yardage is based on 42"-wide fabric, unless otherwise noted.*

10" x 10" square *each* of assorted prints for blocks: at least 6 blue, 3 pink, 2 yellow, and 2 gray*

⅓ yard of cream solid for block backgrounds

⅛ yard of cream print for border

⅛ yard of blue print for binding

½ yard OR 1 fat quarter of fabric for backing

18" x 22" piece of batting

*Precut Layer Cake squares work perfectly for this project.*

### Starch for Stability

It really helps to starch and press all of the fabrics *before* cutting, as the starch provides extra stability when working with small cuts of fabric. When using starch, plan to wash your quilt after it's finished.

## Cutting

*All measurements include ¼"-wide seam allowances.*

**From *each* of the blue, pink, and yellow 10" squares, cut:**
    1 square, 2½" x 2½"
    8 squares, 1½" x 1½"
    2 squares, 2" x 2"

**From 1 gray 10" square, cut:**
    1 square, 2½" x 2½"
    8 squares, 1½" x 1½"

**From another gray 10" square, cut:**
    2 squares, 2" x 2"

**From the cream solid, cut:**
    2 strips, 2" x 42"; crosscut into 24 squares, 2" x 2"
    3 strips, 1½" x 42"; crosscut into 48 rectangles, 1½" x 2½"

**From the cream print, cut:**
    2 strips, 1¾" x 42"; crosscut into:
        2 strips, 1¾" x 16½"
        2 strips, 1¾" x 15"

**From the blue print, cut:**
    2 strips, 2" x 42"

## Make it MARVELOUS
### from Sherri McConnell

As a designer, she's sweet as can be, but as a superhero, Sherri gets really steamed as the *Iron Maven*—a prime presser!

- **My latest marvelous binge is** buying low-volume print fabrics. I can't get enough of them.

- **If I had a three-word mantra, it would be:** Design. Quilt. Repeat.

- **If I were a quilting superhero, my superpower in the sewing room would be** ironing and pressing with the snap of a finger!

- **One reason mini-quilts are fun to make:** Instant gratification!

- **For general piecing, my go-to needle is** size 80/12.

- **On my mini playlist, what I'm listening to now is** Adele's 25.

- **When making a mini-quilt, I'm more likely** to go to my scrap basket for fabrics.

- **Here's a little tip on making it mini:** Starch your fabrics before cutting! (See "Starch for Stability" on page 6.)

## Assembling the Blocks

Instructions are for piecing one block at a time. For each block, you'll need pieces cut from two prints. Sherri used two different prints from the same color:

**Print A:** eight 1½" squares and one 2½" square
**Print B:** two 2" squares
**Cream solid:** two 2" squares and four 1½" x 2½" rectangles

**1** Draw a diagonal line from corner to corner on the wrong side of the eight matching print A 1½" squares. Place a marked square right sides together on one end of a cream 1½" x 2½" rectangle, orienting the line as shown. Sew on the line, and then press the square away from the rectangle. Trim the seam allowances to ¼". Repeat to sew a second marked square on the opposite end of the rectangle to complete a flying-geese unit. Repeat to make four matching units that measure 1½" x 2½".

Make 4.

**2** Draw a diagonal line from corner to corner on the wrong side of two cream 2" squares. Place each marked square right sides together with a print B 2" square. Sew ¼" from each side of the marked lines. Cut along the lines to yield two matching half-square-triangle units from each pair of squares for a total of four. Press the seam allowances toward the print. Trim the units to 1½" square.

  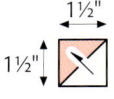

Make 4.

**3** Lay out the print A 2½" square, the four half-square-triangle units, and the four flying-geese units in three rows as shown. Join the units in each row. Press the seam allowances in opposite directions from row to row. Join the rows; press the seam allowances open. The block should measure 4½" square.

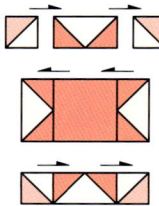 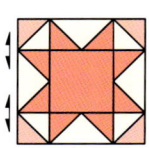

**4** Repeat steps 1–3 to make six blue blocks, three pink blocks, two yellow blocks, and one gray block (12 total).

## Assembling the Quilt Top

**1** Lay out four rows of three blocks each as shown in the quilt assembly diagram below. Join the blocks in each row; press the seam allowances open.

**2** Join the rows; press the seam allowances open.

**3** Sew the white 1¾" x 16½" border strips to the sides of the quilt center; press the seam allowances toward the borders. Sew the remaining border strips to the top and bottom of the quilt; press the seam allowances toward the borders.

## Finishing the Quilt

Go to ShopMartingale.com/HowtoQuilt for more details on quilting and finishing.

**1** Layer the backing, batting, and quilt top; baste the layers together. Hand or machine quilt as desired. The quilt shown was quilted with horizontal cables.

**2** Use the blue 2"-wide strips to make the binding and attach it to the quilt.

### *Opposites are fun!*

Which describes your current status better:

☐ **Streamlined Stash OR Supersized Stash** ☒

☒ **Press Seam Allowances Open OR Press to One Side** ☐

☐ **Salty OR Sweet** ☒

☒ **Steam OR No Steam** ☐

☐ **Prewashing OR No Prewashing** ☒

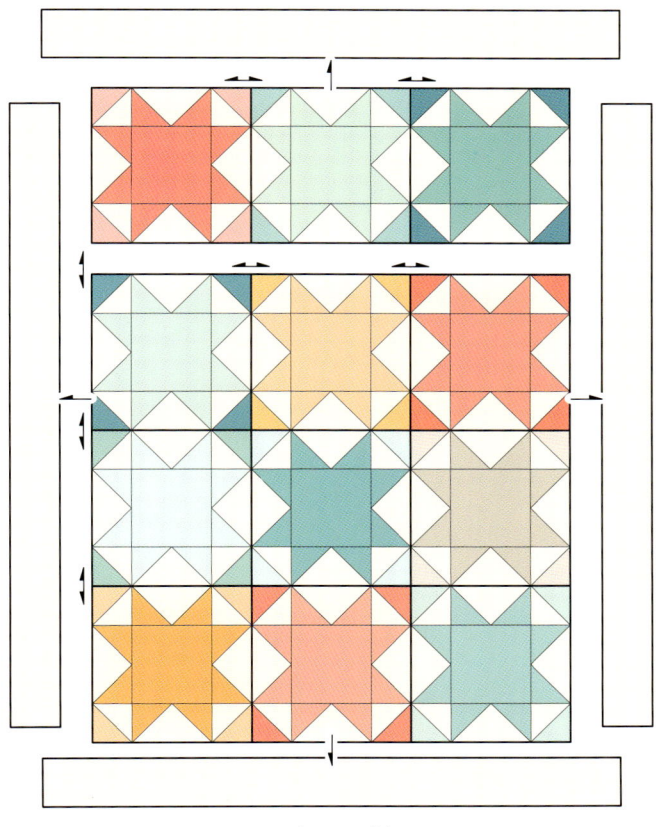

Quilt assembly

# Bee's Knees

*The blocks in this charming mini-quilt combine patchwork and appliqué to resemble little bees buzzing around a blossom.*

Designed and made by Sandy Gervais

**Finished quilt:** 12½" x 12½"

**Finished block:** 3½" x 3½"

## Materials

*Yardage is based on 42"-wide fabric, unless otherwise noted.*

⅓ yard of light-aqua print for bee wings, outer border, and binding

¼ yard of cream solid for blocks and inner border

⅛ yard of orchid solid for blocks and middle border

5" square *each* of 4 assorted teal solids for blocks and bee bodies

½ yard or 1 fat quarter of fabric for backing

⅛ yard of 18"-wide lightweight fusible web

15" x 15" piece of batting

## Cutting

*All measurements include ¼"-wide seam allowances.*

**From *each* teal solid, cut:**
    4 squares, 1" x 1"
    Reserve the remainder for appliqués.

**From the cream solid, cut:**
    2 strips, 1" x 42"; crosscut into:
        16 squares, 1" x 1"
        2 rectangles, 1" x 7½"
        2 rectangles, 1" x 8½"
    2 strips, 1½" x 42"; crosscut into:
        8 rectangles, 1½" x 2"
        8 rectangles, 1½" x 4"

**From the orchid solid, cut:**
    4 squares, 1" x 1"
    2 rectangles, 1" x 8½"
    2 rectangles, 1" x 9½"

**From the light-aqua print, cut:**
    4 strips, 2" x 42"; crosscut *2 of the strips* into:
        2 rectangles, 2" x 9½"
        2 rectangles, 2" x 12½"
    Reserve the remainder for appliqués.

## Make it MARVELOUS
### from Sandy Gervais

Her reputation as an artist and designer is well known. But what's less commonly known is Sandy's superhero status as ***Pinky Scissorhands.*** With the wave of those marvelous hands, she's able to snip the dog-ears off a block and vaporize the tiny clipped-off fabric bits as though they never existed. No muss, no fuss. How's that for super?

- **My latest marvelous binge is** watching Vogue preseason fashion slide shows on the Internet.

- **If I had a three-word mantra, it would be:** Eat more chocolate!

- **If I were a quilting superhero, my superpower in the sewing room would be** having dog-ears disappear into thin air when you trim them off so they don't end up on the sewing-room floor.

- **One reason mini-quilts are fun to make:** They take less time to make, therefore giving you more time to make more quilts.

- **For general piecing, my go-to needle is** size 80/12.

- **On my mini playlist, what I'm listening to now is** nothing. I never listen to music.

- **When making a mini-quilt, I'm more likely** to go to my stash of uncut fabric.

- **Here's a little tip on making it mini:** If you're converting a large-sized quilt pattern that uses 10" squares, but there are pieces that finish at ½", it's best not to try reducing the scale to a mini. I learned this the hard way!

## Making the Blocks

**1** Lay out four matching teal squares, four cream squares, and one orchid square in three rows. Join the squares in each row; press the seam allowances toward the teal and orchid squares. Join the rows; press the seam allowances open. The unit should measure 2" square.

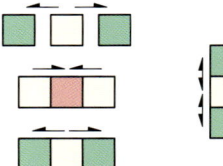
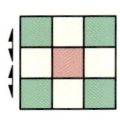

**2** Sew cream 1½" x 2" rectangles to the top and bottom of the nine-patch unit. Press the seam allowances toward the rectangles.

**3** Sew cream 1½" x 4" rectangles to the sides of the unit. Press the seam allowances toward the rectangles. The block should be 4" square.

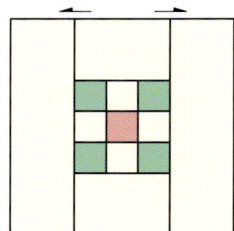

**4** Repeat steps 1–3 to make four blocks.

## Adding the Appliqué

**1** Using the patterns on page 13, trace 32 bee wings and 16 bee bodies onto fusible web. Cut ⅛" outside the edges of each shape.

**2** Fuse all of the bee wings onto the light aqua print and fuse four bodies onto each teal solid following the manufacturer's instructions. Allow to cool; then cut out the shapes exactly along the drawn lines. Peel the paper away from the appliqués.

**3** Referring to the diagram on the facing page for placement, position the bee wings and matching teal bee bodies on the blocks and fuse in place. The edges of the appliqués on the featured quilt were left raw. If you need more information, download free appliqué instructions at ShopMartingale.com/HowtoQuilt.

## Assembling the Quilt Top

1 Lay out the four blocks as shown in the quilt assembly diagram below. Join the blocks in each row; press the seam allowances open. Join the rows; press the seam allowances open. The quilt center should be 7½" square.

2 Sew the cream 1" x 7½" border strips to the top and bottom of the quilt center; press the seam allowances toward the borders. Sew the remaining cream strips to the sides of the quilt; press. Sew the orchid and aqua border strips to the edges of the quilt in the same manner; press.

## Finishing the Quilt

Go to ShopMartingale.com/HowtoQuilt for more details on quilting and finishing.

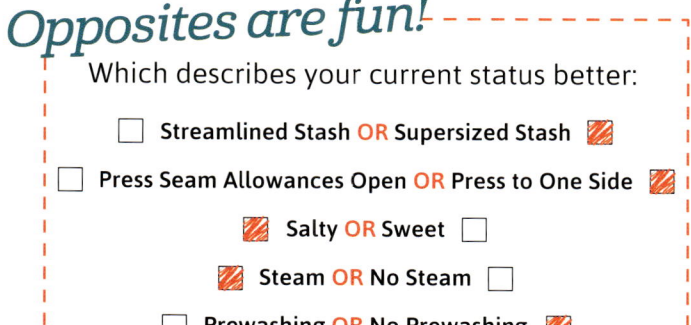

## Opposites are fun!

Which describes your current status better:

☐ Streamlined Stash OR Supersized Stash ▨

☐ Press Seam Allowances Open OR Press to One Side ▨

▨ Salty OR Sweet ☐

▨ Steam OR No Steam ☐

☐ Prewashing OR No Prewashing ▨

1 Layer the backing, batting, and quilt top; baste the layers together. Hand or machine quilt as desired. The quilt shown was simply quilted in the ditch around the blocks and borders to add dimension.

2 Use the remaining aqua 2"-wide strips to make the binding and attach it to the quilt.

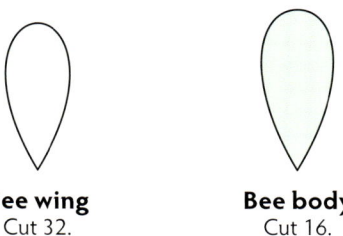

**Bee wing**
Cut 32.

**Bee body**
Cut 16.

Appliqué patterns do not include seam allowances.

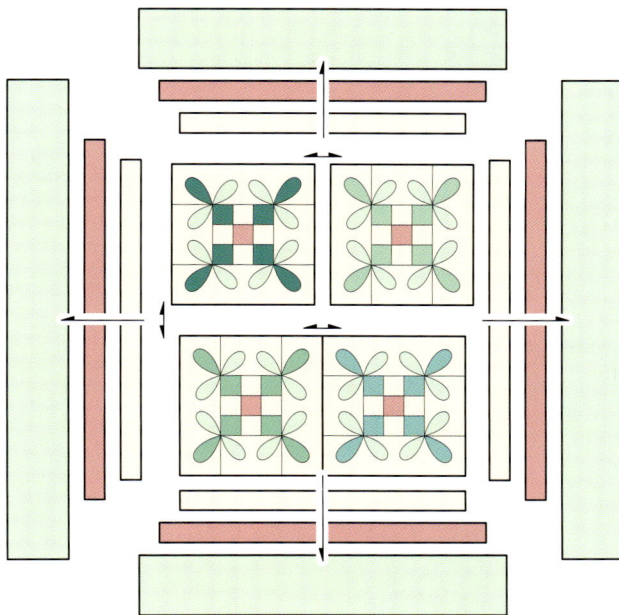

Quilt assembly

# Cabin Skein

*You may have heard of a gaggle of geese, but this quilt is named for geese in flight, also known as a skein. Delve into your scrap basket to make this showstopping quilt featuring small versions of classic Log Cabin blocks and flying-geese units.*

Designed and made by Carrie Nelson
**Finished quilt:** 20½" x 20½"
**Finished blocks:** 4" x 4"

## Materials

*Yardage is based on 42"-wide fabric, unless otherwise noted.*

8 squares, 10" x 10", of assorted dark prints*

8 squares, 10" x 10", of assorted light prints*

¼ yard of gray homespun for binding

¾ yard of fabric for backing

23" x 23" piece of batting

*Precut Layer Cake squares work perfectly for this project. Use more than eight prints to achieve a scrappier look.*

## Cutting

*All measurements include ¼"-wide seam allowances.*

**From the assorted dark prints, cut:**
20 squares, 3¼" x 3¼"
16 squares, 1½" x 1½"
36 *lengthwise* strips, 1" x 10"; crosscut into:
  16 rectangles, 1" x 4½"
  16 rectangles, 1" x 4"
  16 rectangles, 1" x 3½"
  16 rectangles, 1" x 3"
  16 rectangles, 1" x 2½"
  16 rectangles, 1" x 2"

**From the assorted light prints, cut:**
64 squares, 1⅞" x 1⅞"
34 *lengthwise* strips, 1" x 10"; crosscut into:
  16 rectangles, 1" x 4"
  16 rectangles, 1" x 3½"
  16 rectangles, 1" x 3"
  16 rectangles, 1" x 2½"
  16 rectangles, 1" x 2"
  16 rectangles, 1" x 1½"

**From the gray homespun, cut:**
3 strips, 2¼" x 42"

### Stop the Stretch

Cut the rectangles for the Log Cabin blocks along the *lengthwise* grain to prevent stretching and distortion as you sew them. This helps keep the seams accurate and the block tidy and square. To determine the lengthwise grain, gently stretch the 10" squares; the lengthwise grain will have little or no stretch and the crosswise grain will have more give.

## Make it
# MARVELOUS
### from Carrie Nelson

A designer who wears many hats by day, Carrie's got a rosy outlook on the future, but what few know is that her sewing superpower is hindsight! That's right, **Baby Got Back-Eyes** has super shoulda-woulda-coulda powers.

- **My latest marvelous binge is** supercool stacking storage boxes at IKEA, called Kuggis. They're inexpensive and two of the smaller stack perfectly side-by-side on the larger one. They *rock!*

- **If I had a three-word mantra, it would be:** This too shall pass. (I know, it's four words.)

- **If I were a quilting superhero, my superpower in the sewing room would be** hindsight! I'd have bought and stashed as much early American Jane and Bonnie & Camille fabrics as humanly possible!

- **One reason mini-quilts are fun to make:** You can make something different without investing a fortune or a lifetime making it.

- **For general piecing, my go-to needle is** size 75/11 Universal. With finer threads like Aurifil and Presencia 60-weight, these needles do the best job with my old sewing machines.

- **On my mini playlist, what I'm listening to now is** anything by Mumford & Sons and Adele. The top three songs on my playlist are "Renegades" by X Ambassadors, "Hello" by Adele, and "Tompkins Square Park" by Mumford & Sons.

- **When making a mini-quilt, I'm more likely** to use a Layer Cake or some charm packs from my stash.

- **Here's a little tip on making it mini:** Perfection is overrated; enjoying the process is what matters.

## Making the Log Cabin Blocks

Press all seam allowances toward the rectangle just added.

1 Sew one light 1" x 1½" rectangle to the bottom of a dark 1½" square; press.

2 Sew a light 1" x 2" rectangle to the left side of the square; press. Sew a dark 1" x 2" rectangle to the top edge and press. Sew a dark 1" x 2½" rectangle to the right side; press.

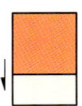

3 Continue rotating the unit and adding rectangles in size order as shown, creating the light/dark pattern. Add two more rounds until the block is 4½" square.

Make 16.

4 Repeat steps 1–3 to make a total of 16 Log Cabin blocks.

## Making the Quarter-Square-Triangle Units

1 Select four different dark 3¼" squares. Draw a diagonal line from corner to corner on the wrong side of two squares. Pair each marked square right sides together with an unmarked square. Sew a scant ¼" from both sides of the marked lines. Cut along the marked lines to yield four half-square-triangle units; press the seam allowances toward the darker fabric. Each half-square triangle should measure 2⅞" square.

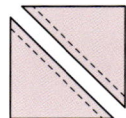

**2** Draw a diagonal line perpendicular to the seam on the wrong side of one half-square-triangle unit. Place the marked unit right sides together with a second half-square-triangle unit, placing the seams perpendicular to each other. Sew a scant ¼" from both sides of the marked line. Cut along the line to yield two quarter-square-triangle units; press the seam allowances in one direction. Each quarter-square-triangle unit should measure 2½" square. Make four quarter-square-triangle units for the sashing cornerstones.

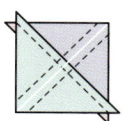  

Make 4.

## Making the Flying-Geese Units

**1** Draw a diagonal line from corner to corner to corner on the wrong sides of the light 1⅞" squares. Place two marked squares on opposite corners of one large dark square, right sides together as shown. Sew a scant ¼" from both sides of the drawn line.

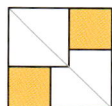 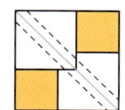

**2** Cut the unit along the drawn line to yield two units. Press the seam allowances toward the light triangles.

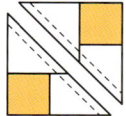 

**3** Place a marked light 1⅞" square with right sides together on the corner of each pressed unit, orienting the line as shown. Sew a scant ¼" from both sides of the line. Cut along the drawn line to yield two flying-geese units. Press toward the light fabric.

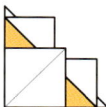  

**4** Repeat steps 1–3 to make a total of 64 flying-geese units.

**5** Lay out four flying-geese units in a row, pointing the same direction. Join the units; press the seam allowances open. Make 16 flying-geese sashing rows. Each sashing row should measure 2½" x 4½".

Make 16.

### Opposites are fun!

Which describes your current status better:

☑ **Streamlined Stash OR Supersized Stash** ☑
(Both. Not either. It used to be supersized, now it's just "healthy," but it's getting leaner with each move. And another evaluation is in the works)

☑ **Press Seam Allowances Open OR Press to One Side** ☑
(Both. It depends on the seam, the block, the fabric and what's happening with that particular seam. That said, my first inclination is to one side.)

☑ **Salty OR Sweet** ☐

☑ **Steam OR No Steam** ☐

☐ **Prewashing OR No Prewashing** ☐
(Neither—I don't prewash, but I always prep with sizing starch to shrink the fabric, which also tests the colorfastness of the fabric at the same time.)

## Assembling the Quilt Top

**1** Arrange four Log Cabin blocks, four flying-geese rows, and one sashing cornerstone in three rows as shown. Orient the light side of the Log Cabin blocks to the outside edges. Join the units in each row; press the seam allowances open. Join the rows; press. Make four.

Make 4.

**2** Lay out the units from step 1 in two rows of two. Sew together in rows; press the seam allowances open. Join the rows; press.

## Finishing the Quilt

Go to ShopMartingale.com/HowtoQuilt for more details on quilting and finishing.

**1** Layer the backing, batting, and quilt top; baste the layers together. Hand or machine quilt as desired. The quilt shown was machine quilted with straight parallel lines, reminiscent of stacked logs.

**2** Use the gray homespun 2¼"-wide strips to make the binding and attach it to the quilt.

Quilt assembly

# Little Love

## Materials

Yardage is based on 42"-wide fabric. Fat quarters measure approximately 18" x 21"; fat eighths are 9" x 21".

20 squares, 2½" x 2½", of assorted light prints for blocks*

20 squares, 2½" x 2½", of assorted dark prints for blocks*

1 fat eighth of red print for binding

1 fat quarter for backing

¼ yard of 18"-wide lightweight fusible web

11" x 14" piece of batting

*Precut mini charm squares work perfectly for this project.

## Cutting

All measurements include ¼"-wide seam allowances.

**From the red print for binding, cut:**
3 strips, 2½" x 21"

*Make a sweet mini that's big on romance. This adorable quilt comes together so quickly that you'll want to make one for everyone you love.*

Designed and quilted by Edyta Sitar
**Finished quilt: 8½" x 10½"**
**Finished block: 2" x 2"**

Able to bring together sewing buddies with a sweeping glance around the globe, Edyta's superhero persona is a PHD (pretty happy designer) known as **DOCTOR ALLTOGETHERNOW.**

- **My latest marvelous binge is** watching *Fixer Upper* on HGTV.

- **If I had a three-word mantra, it would be:** Love, love, love.

- **If I were a quilting superhero, my superpower in the sewing room would be** the ability to transport my friends to my location so that we could quilt together.

- **One reason mini-quilts are fun to make:** They are small and you can complete them quickly and then give them to someone with a little bit of love.

- **For general piecing, my go-to needle is** a Microtex size 70/10.

- **On my mini playlist, what I'm listening to now is** Fleetwood Mac.

- **When making a mini-quilt, I'm more likely** to go to my scrap basket for fabrics or use mini charms.

- **Here's a little tip on making it mini:** Don't stress—you can always make another one!

## Appliquéing the Blocks

**1** Using the pattern on page 22, trace 20 hearts onto the paper side of the fusible web. Cut ⅛" outside the edges of each heart.

**2** Fuse each heart onto the wrong side of 19 dark squares and one light square following the manufacturer's instructions. Allow to cool; then cut out the hearts exactly along the drawn lines. Peel the paper away from the hearts.

**3** Center and fuse a dark heart onto each of the 19 light squares. Center and fuse the light heart onto the remaining dark square. Sew the edges of the hearts using your preferred hand- or machine-appliqué stitch. The appliqués on Edyta's quilt were attached with a small machine blanket stitch in coordinating thread colors. For more information, you can download free fusible-appliqué instructions at ShopMartingale.com/HowtoQuilt.

Make 19.

Make 1.

## Assembling the Quilt Top

Lay out the blocks in five rows of four each, placing the square with the light heart in the second row from the bottom. Join the blocks in each row; press the seam allowances in opposite directions from row to row. Join the rows; press the seam allowances in one direction.

Quilt assembly

## Finishing the Quilt

Go to ShopMartingale.com/HowtoQuilt for more details on quilting and finishing.

1 Layer the backing, batting, and quilt top; baste the layers together. Hand or machine quilt as desired. The quilt shown was machine quilted in the ditch around the blocks to add dimension.

2 Use the red 2½"-wide print strips to make the binding and attach it to the quilt.

**Heart**
Cut 20.

Appliqué pattern does not include seam allowances.

## Opposites *are fun!*

Which describes your current status better:

- ☑ Streamlined Stash **OR** Supersized Stash ☐
- ☐ Press Seam Allowances Open **OR** Press to One Side ☑
- ☐ Salty **OR** Sweet ☑
- ☑ Steam **OR** No Steam ☐
- ☐ Prewashing **OR** No Prewashing ☑

# Dashing

## Materials

Yardage is based on 42"-wide fabric.

½ yard of navy print for blocks, setting triangles, and binding

¼ yard of tan print for blocks

13 squares, 5" x 5", of assorted prints for blocks*

⅝ yard of fabric for backing

22" x 22" piece of batting

Fabric glue stick

*Precut charm squares work perfectly for this project.

## Cutting

All measurements include ¼"-wide seam allowances.

**From each of the assorted print 5" squares, cut:**
    1 square, 1¼" x 1¼" (13 total)
    2 squares, 1½" x 1½"; cut each square in half
        diagonally to yield 4 triangles (52 total)

**From the navy print, cut:**
    2 strips, 2" x 42"; crosscut into:
        16 squares, 2" x 2"
        16 rectangles, 1¼" x 2"
    2 squares, 7" x 7", cut each square in quarters
        diagonally to yield 8 triangles
    2 squares, 4" x 4", cut each square in half
        diagonally to yield 4 triangles
    2 strips, 2¼" x 42"

**From the tan print, cut:**
    3 strips, 2" x 42"; crosscut into:
        36 squares, 2" x 2"
        36 rectangles, 1¼" x 2"

*Set small Churn Dash blocks on point in this quick-to-make quilt. Lynne's clever technique, called Layered Patchwork, is a bit like raw-edge appliqué. You'll have these cute, cozy blocks pieced in a flash.*

Designed and pieced by Lynne Hagmeier; quilted by Joy Johnson

**Finished size:** 16½" x 16½"
**Finished block:** 3¾" x 3¾"

Kansas Troubles Quilters may be the name by which you know Lynne best, but her super sewing buddies know her as **Speedy Von Piecer,** able to do fast-paced patchwork piecing.

- **My latest marvelous binge is** a wonderful vintage quilt.

- **If I had a three-word mantra, it would be:** Do better tomorrow.

- **If I were a quilting superhero, my superpower in the sewing room would be** superfast piecing.

- **One reason mini-quilts are fun to make:** Major fun in mini time.

- **For general piecing, my go-to needle is** a Schmetz size 70/10 Sharp.

- **On my mini playlist, what I'm listening to now is** "Happy" by Pharrell Williams, "Just Give Me a Reason," by Pink, and anything by Adele.

- **When making a mini-quilt, I'm more likely to** go to my scrap basket for fabric. Definitely scraps!

- **Here's a little tip on making it mini:** Cut precisely.

## Assembling the Blocks

**1** Select a print triangle that contrasts with the navy print and layer it over one corner of a navy 2" square with right sides facing up, aligning the edges. Working on the wrong side of the fabric, apply small swipes of fabric glue at the two points of the triangle's long edge. The glue will hold the points in place as you stitch across the bias. (There's no need to glue the bottom point of the triangle.) Stitch 1⁄8" from the triangle's raw bias edge using cotton thread in a coordinating color. Sew each of the three remaining matching triangles on a navy square to make four. Each should still be 2" square.

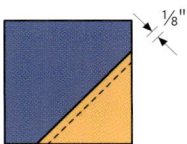

Make 4.

**2** Lay out the four 2" layered squares, four navy 1¼" x 2" rectangles, and the matching print 1¼" square in three rows as shown. Join the units in each row. Press the seam allowances in the top and bottom row toward the squares. Press the seam allowances of the center row toward the center square. Join the rows; press the seam allowances toward the top and bottom rows. The block should measure 4¼" square. Make four navy blocks.

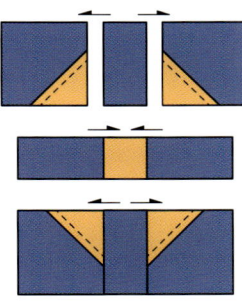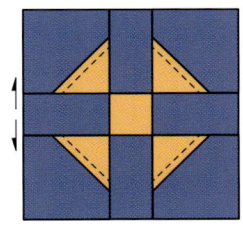

Make 4.

**3** Repeat steps 1 and 2 to make the tan blocks in the same manner as the navy blocks, but press the seam allowances in the opposite directions. Make nine tan blocks.

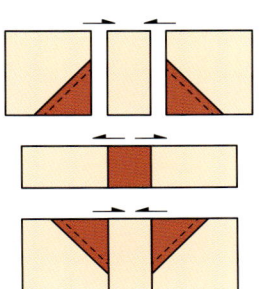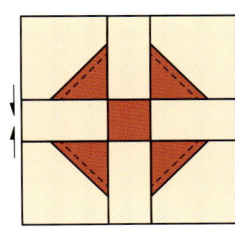

Make 9.

## Assembling the Quilt Top

**1** Lay out the blocks on point in diagonal rows as shown in the quilt assembly diagram below. Place the navy 7" setting triangles along the outer edges. Note that the corner and side setting triangles are cut slightly oversized and will be trimmed after assembly.

**2** Join the blocks and side setting triangles in each row. Press the seam allowances in opposite directions from row to row. Join the rows; press the seam allowances in one direction. Add a navy 4" triangle to each corner; press the seam allowances toward the triangles.

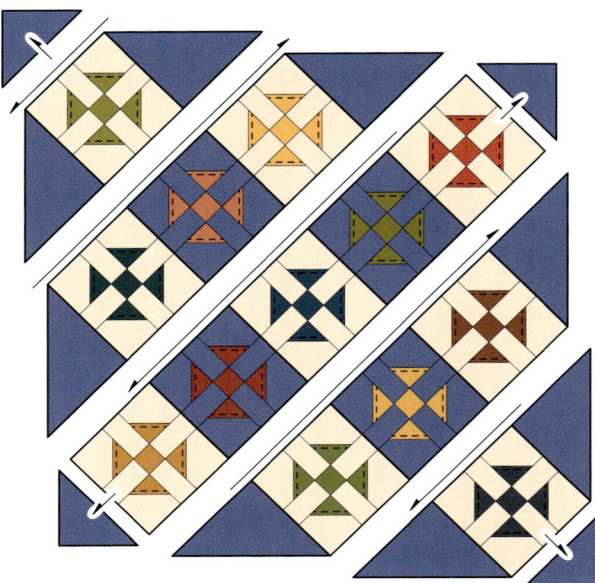

Quilt assembly

**3** Square the quilt top, trimming the edges of the setting and corner triangles to allow ¼" beyond the block points.

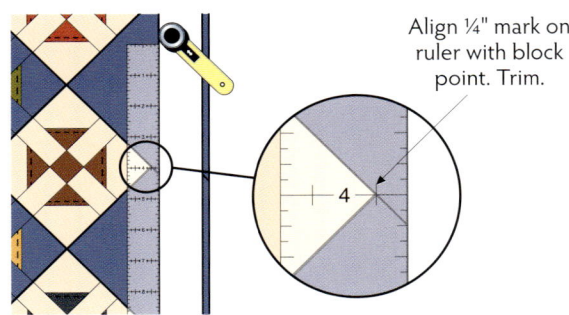

Align ¼" mark on ruler with block point. Trim.

## Finishing the Quilt

Go to ShopMartingale.com/HowtoQuilt for more details on quilting and finishing.

**1** Layer the backing, batting, and quilt top; baste the layers together. Hand or machine quilt as desired. The quilt shown was machine quilted in a lattice pattern to emphasize the on-point setting.

**2** Use the navy 2¼"-wide strips to make the binding and attach it to the quilt.

## Opposites are fun!

Which describes your current status better:

☐ **Streamlined Stash OR Supersized Stash** ☒

☐ **Press Seam Allowances Open OR Press to One Side** ☒

☒ **Salty OR Sweet** ☐

☒ **Steam OR No Steam** ☐

☐ **Prewashing OR No Prewashing** ☒

# Butterfly Kisses

*Pat's inspiration for this fun appliqué quilt came from the butterfly bush she planted next to her front porch. She's seen up to a dozen butterflies visiting at once—truly magical!*

Designed and made by Pat Sloan

**Finished size:** 16½" x 16½"

**Finished block:** 8" x 8"

## Materials

*Yardage is based on 42"-wide fabric. Fat eighths measure approximately 9" x 21".*

1 fat eighth *each* of 2 light prints for block backgrounds

⅛ yard of white-on-black large polka dot for wings*

⅛ yard of white-on-black small polka dot for wings*

⅛ yard of black-on-white small polka dot for wings*

1 square, 5" x 5" *each*, of 4 hot-pink prints for wings

1 square, 5" x 5", of black stripe for body

¼ yard of pink tone on tone for binding

⅝ yard of fabric for backing

22" x 22" piece of batting

½ yard of 18"-wide lightweight fusible web

*Or 1 fat eighth

## Cutting

*All measurements include ¼"-wide seam allowances. Use the patterns on page 31 and refer to "Appliquéing the Blocks" on page 29 to prepare the shapes for fusible appliqué.*

**From *each* light print fat eighth, cut:**
2 squares, 9" x 9"*

**From the white-on-black large-scale polka dot, cut:**
4 of left wing A
4 of right wing A

**From the white-on-black small-scale polka dot, cut:**
4 of left wing C
4 of right wing C

**From the black-on-white small-scale polka dot, cut:**
4 of left wing D
4 of right wing D

**From *each* pink square, cut:**
1 of left wing B
1 of right wing B

**From the black stripe, cut:**
4 bodies

**From the pink tone on tone, cut:**
2 strips, 2½" x 42"

*If your fat eighth is a little too narrow to cut a 9" square, don't worry; you'll be trimming these squares down to 8½" after adding the appliqué.*

*"It's a square! It's a triangle! It's a half-square triangle!"* That's the chant of designer Pat Sloan when she's got her superhero suit on as **The Triangler.** Sewing dozens of half-square triangles in a single sewing session at a terrifically triumphant speed is a cinch for her!

- **My latest marvelous binge is** a holiday-flavored latte every single day for a week. The flavor leaves the coffee shop after the holidays, so I love this treat while it lasts.

- **If I had a three-word mantra, it would be:** Let's go sew!

- **If I were a quilting superhero, my superpower in the sewing room would be** the ability to trim half-square triangles to size at the speed of sound (see my triangle book, *Pat Sloan's Teach Me to Sew Triangles,* for a trick!).

- **One reason mini-quilts are fun to make:** Everything is better when it's teeny-tiny. Small is adorable!

- **For general piecing, my go-to needle is** size 80/12.

- **On my mini playlist, what I'm listening to now is** birds in my yard, the sound of the ocean, and the fire engines on my back road (I don't own a playlist!).

- **When making a mini-quilt, I'm more likely** to go to my stash of uncut fabric every single time. Scraps are for scrap quilts!

- **Here's a little tip on making it mini:** Check the scale/size of your fabric prints for the shape you're making. I love large prints, but a mini-quilt might need a small-scale print to make it wonderful!

## Appliquéing the Blocks

1 Using the patterns on page 31, trace four of each appliqué shape onto the paper side of the fusible web. Cut ⅛" outside the edges of each shape.

2 Fuse each shape onto the wrong side of the appropriate pink and polka-dot fabrics. Allow to cool; then cut out the shapes exactly along the drawn lines. Peel the paper away from the pieces.

3 Fold the light squares in half in both directions and finger press to mark the block center with a crease as a guide. Position the left and right A and C wings on one of the light squares and fuse in place.

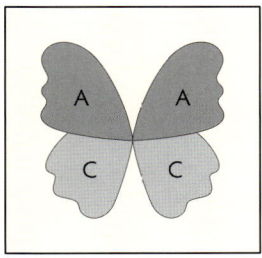

4 Postion and fuse the B wings to the A wings and the D wings to the C wings. Then place the body between the wings and fuse. Pat blanket-stitched by machine around each shape using matching thread. If you need more information, you can download free appliqué instructions at ShopMartingale.com/HowtoQuilt or check out Pat's book, *Pat Sloan's Teach Me to Appliqué.*

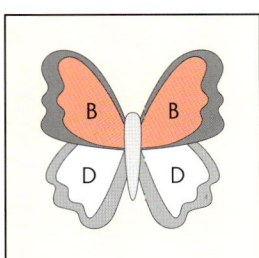

5 Repeat to make four appliquéd blocks. Trim the blocks to measure 8½" square. The butterfly antennae were free-motion quilted with black thread. If you prefer, embroider the lines before trimming the blocks using black embroidery floss and a backstitch (see "Embroidery Stitches" on page 79).

## Assembling the Quilt Top

Lay out the blocks in two rows of two blocks each. Join the blocks in each row; press the seam allowances in opposite directions. Join the rows; press the seam allowances in one direction.

Quilt assembly

## Finishing the Quilt

Go to ShopMartingale.com/HowtoQuilt for more details on quilting and finishing.

1 Layer the backing, batting, and quilt top; baste the layers together.

2 Hand or machine quilt as desired. The quilt shown was machine quilted with a variety of shapes to showcase the design and add interest to the appliqués. The upper wings of the butterfly were highlighted with free-motion curved lines, and the lower wings were quilted with echoing lines. The antennae of the butterflies were free-motion quilted with black thread, and the background of the blocks was quilted with an allover loop design.

3 Use the pink 2½"-wide strips to make the binding and attach it to the quilt. Pat attached the binding to the *back* of her quilt and then used a machine blanket stitch to attach the binding to the front.

## *Opposites are fun!*

Which describes your current status better:

[✓] Streamlined Stash **OR** Supersized Stash [ ]

[ ] Press Seam Allowances Open **OR** Press to One Side [✓]

[✓] Salty **OR** Sweet [ ]

[✓] Steam **OR** No Steam [ ]

[ ] Prewashing **OR** No Prewashing [✓]

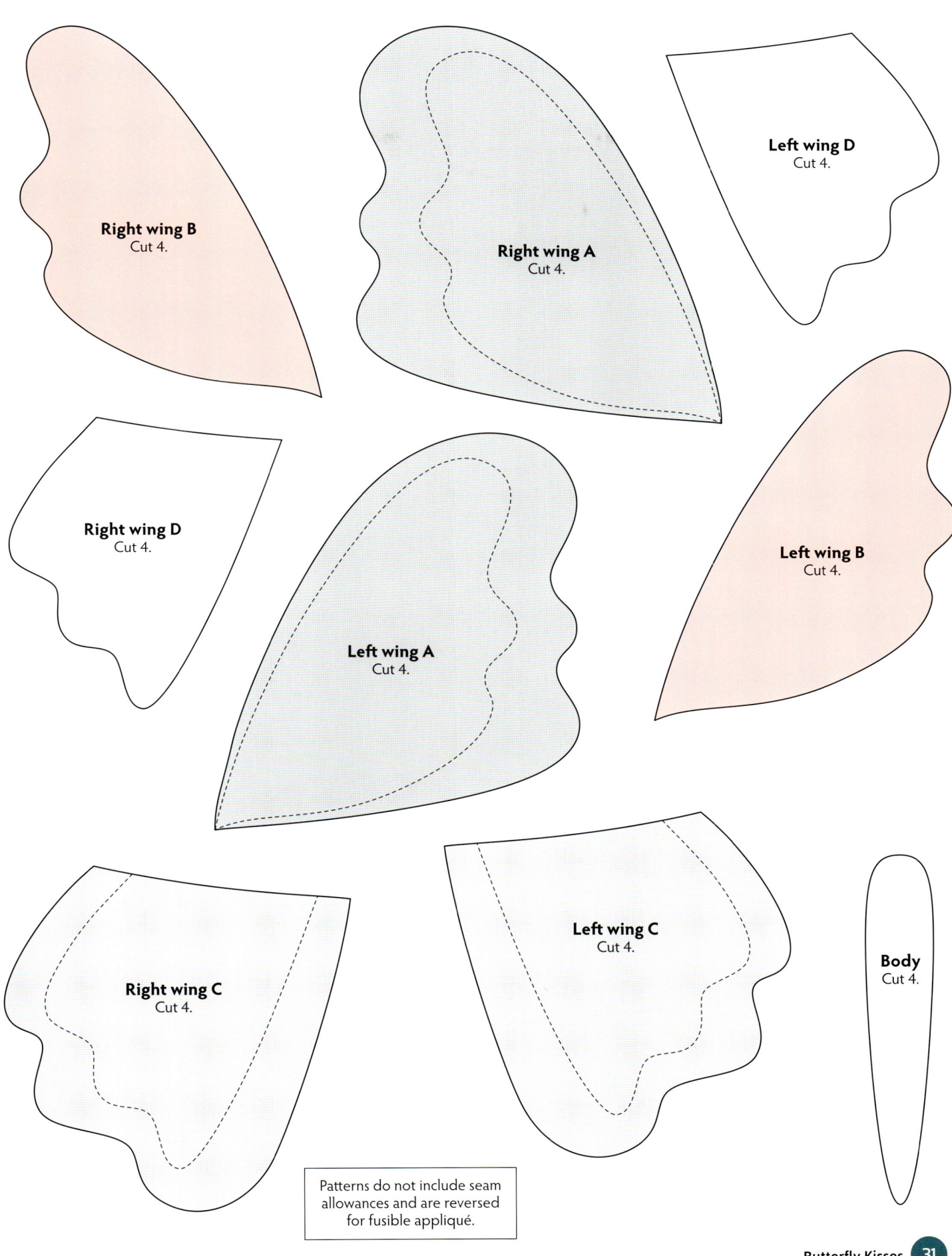

Right wing B
Cut 4.

Right wing A
Cut 4.

Left wing D
Cut 4.

Right wing D
Cut 4.

Left wing A
Cut 4.

Left wing B
Cut 4.

Right wing C
Cut 4.

Left wing C
Cut 4.

Body
Cut 4.

Patterns do not include seam allowances and are reversed for fusible appliqué.

# Zen Chic

An ultramodern mini features interlocking rectangles that form an intriguing composition. The slate-gray background perfectly complements the bright prints.

Designed and made by Brigitte Heitland
**Finished Quilt:** 16½" x 16½"

## Materials

*Yardage is based on 42"-wide fabric. Scrap sizes are approximate.*

⅓ yard of dark gray print for background

2½" x 16" scrap of aqua print for patchwork

2½" x 16" scrap of coral print for patchwork

1½" x 16" scrap of green print #1 for patchwork

1½" x 12" scrap of orange print #1 for patchwork

3" x 4" scrap *each* of 4 pink prints (#1–4) for patchwork

2" x 3" scrap *each* of 2 light gray prints (#1 and #2) for patchwork

2" x 2" scrap of green print #2 for patchwork

2" x 2" scrap of orange print #2 for patchwork

¼ yard of light-gray print for binding

⅝ yard of fabric for backing

21" x 21" piece of batting

## Cutting

*All measurements include ¼"-wide seam allowances.*

**From the dark gray print, cut:**
    1 strip, 2½" x 42"; crosscut into:
        2 rectangles, 2½" x 6½"
        2 rectangles, 2½" x 4½"
        2 rectangles, 2½" x 3½"
        2 squares, 2½" x 2½"
        1 rectangle, 1½" x 2½"
    1 strip, 5½" x 42"; crosscut into:
        1 rectangle, 5½" x 7½"
        1 square, 5½" x 5½"
        1 square, 4½" x 4½"
        1 rectangle, 3½" x 8½"
        1 rectangle, 1½" x 8½"
        1 rectangle, 1½" x 4½"
        1 square, 1½" x 1½"

**From orange print #1, cut:**
    1 square, 1½" x 1½"
    1 rectangle, 1½" x 3½"
    1 rectangle, 1½" x 4½"

**From orange print #2, cut:**
    1 square, 1½" x 1½"

**From pink print #1, cut:**
    1 rectangle, 1½" x 2½"

*Continued on page 34*

*Continued from page 32*

**From pink print #2, cut:**
1 square, 1½" x 1½"

**From pink print #3, cut:**
1 rectangle, 1½" x 2½"

**From pink print #4, cut:**
1 rectangle, 2½" x 3½"

**From the coral print, cut:**
1 rectangle, 2½" x 6½"
1 rectangle, 1½" x 2½"
1 square, 2½" x 2½"
1 rectangle, 2½" x 3½"

**From green print #1, cut:**
2 rectangles, 1½" x 2½"
1 rectangle, 1½" x 4½"
1 rectangle, 1½" x 3½"
1 square, 1½" x 1½"

**From green print #2, cut:**
1 square, 1½" x 1½"

**From light-gray print #1, cut:**
1 rectangle, 1½" x 2½"

**From light-gray print #2, cut:**
1 square, 1½" x 1½"

**From the aqua print, cut:**
1 square, 2½" x 2½"
1 rectangle, 1½" x 3½"
2 squares, 1½" x 1½"
1 rectangle, 2½" x 6½"

**From the light-gray print, cut:**
2 strips, 2¼" x 42"

## Assembling the Sections

The quilt is assembled in four sections. Press seam allowances after sewing each seam, following the arrows in the diagrams.

### Section 1

**1** Sew a dark gray 2½" square to the left side of the coral 2½" x 6½" rectangle. Sew the dark gray 3½" x 8½" rectangle to the top of the unit. The pieced unit should measure 5½" x 8½".

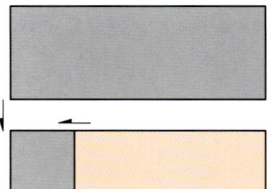

**2** Sew the 1½" orange #1 square to the top of the 1½" x 2½" pink #1 rectangle. Sew a dark gray 2½" x 3½" rectangle to the right side of the unit. Sew the 1½" x 3½" orange #1 rectangle to the right side, and then sew the 1½" x 4½" orange #1 rectangle to the top. Sew the dark gray 4½" square to the right side and the dark gray 1½" x 8½" rectangle to the top. The pieced unit should be 5½" x 8½".

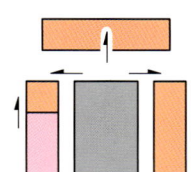
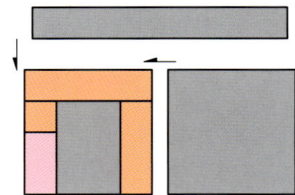

**3** Sew the unit from step 1 to the unit from step 2 to complete section 1. Section 1 should be 5½" x 16½".

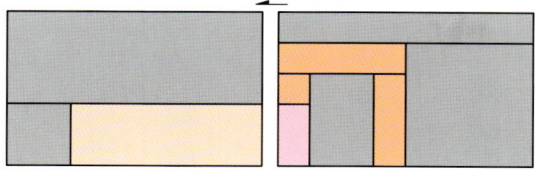

Section 1

## Section 2

**1** Sew the coral 2½" square to the left side of the remaining dark gray 2½" x 3½" rectangle. Sew the coral 1½" x 2½" rectangle to the right side.

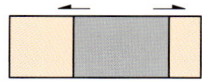

**2** Sew the coral 2½" x 3½" rectangle to the left side of a 2½" x 3½" pink #4 rectangle.

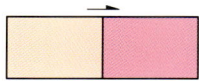

**3** Sew the unit from step 2 to the bottom of the unit from step 1. Add a dark gray 2½" x 4½" rectangle to the left side. The pieced unit should be 4½" x 8½".

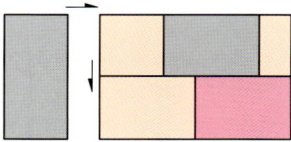

**4** Sew the 1½" square of light gray #2 to the top of the 1½" pink #2 square. Then add the 1½" x 2½" pink #3 rectangle to the bottom.

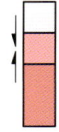

**5** Sew the 1½" x 2½" light gray #1 rectangle to the top of the dark gray 1½" x 2½" rectangle. Add the aqua 2½" square to the bottom.

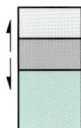

**6** Referring to the diagram below, join the three pieced units from steps 3–5 to make section 2. Section 2 should measure 4½" x 11½".

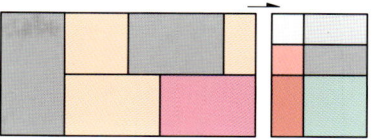

Section 2

## Section 3

**1** Sew the 1½" square of green #1 to the left side of the dark gray 1½" square. Sew the 1½" x 2½" green #1 rectangle to the bottom, and then sew this unit to the right of the remaining dark gray 2½" square. Sew the dark gray 1½" x 4½" rectangle to the bottom of the unit and the aqua 1½" x 3½" rectangle to the left side.

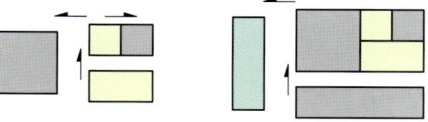

**2** Sew aqua 1½" squares to the top and bottom of the 1½" green #2 square. Sew this unit to the right side of the unit from step 1.

**3** Sew the aqua 2½" x 6½" rectangle to the top of a dark gray 2½" x 6½" rectangle.

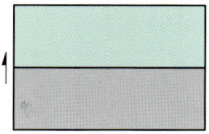

**4** Referring to the diagram below, sew the unit from step 3 to the bottom of the previous unit. Sew the dark gray 5½" x 7½" rectangle to the left side to complete section 3, which should measure 7½" x 11½".

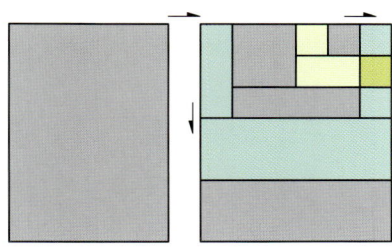

Section 3

## Section 4

**1** Sew the 1½" orange #2 square to the left side of the remaining 1½" x 2½" green #1 rectangle.

**2** Sew the remaining dark gray 2½" x 4½" rectangle to the left side of the 1½" x 4½" green #1 rectangle. Sew the 1½" x 3½" green #1 rectangle to the bottom.

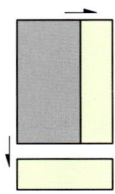

**3** Sew the unit from step 2 to the bottom of the unit from step 1. The unit should be 3½" x 6½". Then sew the remaining dark gray 2½" x 6½" rectangle to the right side and the dark gray 5½" square to the bottom as shown to complete section 4, which should be 5½" x 11½".

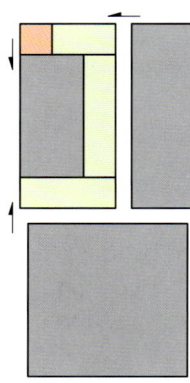

Section 4

## Assembling the Quilt Top

**1** Referring to the assembly diagram below, arrange the four sections as shown.

**2** Sew sections 2 and 3 together. Press all seam allowances as indicated by the arrows.

**3** Sew section 4 to the right side of sections 2 and 3, and then sew section 1 to the top. Press.

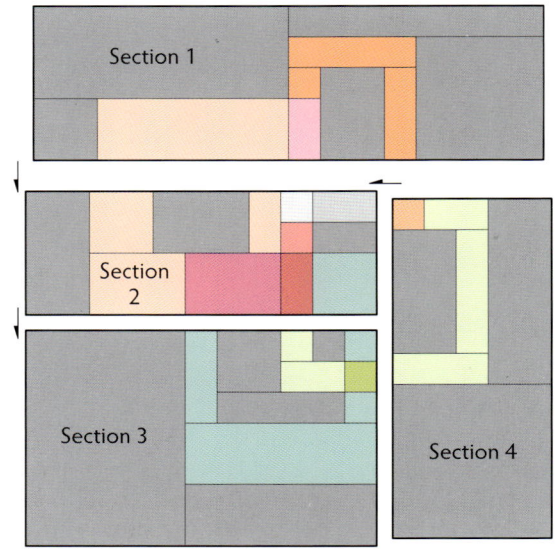

Quilt assembly

## Finishing the Quilt

Go to ShopMartingale.com/HowtoQuilt for more details on quilting and finishing.

**1** Layer the backing, batting, and quilt top; baste the layers together. Hand or machine quilt as desired. The quilt shown was machine quilted in horizontal parallel lines, leaving the bright rectangles unquilted.

**2** Use the light-gray 2¼"-wide strips to make the binding and attach it to the quilt.

## Opposites are fun!

Which describes your current status better:

▨ Streamlined Stash **OR** Supersized Stash ☐

☐ Press Seam Allowances Open **OR** Press to One Side ▨

☐ Salty **OR** Sweet ▨

▨ Steam **OR** No Steam ☐

☐ Prewashing **OR** No Prewashing ▨

# Geese Crossing

*Stitch a simple mini made from three rows of flying geese. Use ombre fabric to create a gradient effect.*

Designed and made by Vanessa Christenson

**Finished size:** 12½" x 12½"

**Finished block:** 2" x 4"

## Materials

*Yardage is based on 42"-wide fabric. Fat eighths measure approximately 9" x 21".*

1 fat eighth *each* of taupe ombre and pink ombre fabrics for blocks

⅓ yard of aqua ombre fabric for blocks and binding

⅓ yard of sand ombre fabric for blocks

1 fat quarter of fabric for backing

17" x 17" square of batting

## Cutting

*All measurements include ¼"-wide seam allowances. To cut ombre fabric, cut the strips perpendicular to the selvage edge, and then crosscut the pieces from the strips to get the full range of dark and light pieces. See "Cutting the Ombre Fabric" on page 39 for helpful tips.*

**From *each* of the taupe and pink ombre fabrics, cut:**
1 strip, 4½" x 21"; crosscut 6 rectangles, 2½" x 4½"

**From the sand fabric, cut:**
3 strips, 2½" x 42"; crosscut 36 squares, 2½" x 2½"

**From the aqua fabric, cut:**
1 strip, 4½" x 42"; crosscut 6 rectangles, 2½" x 4½"
2 strips, 2" x 42"

## Cutting the Ombre Fabric

To get the most variation in color shading from the 4½"-wide ombre strips cut for the Flying Geese rectangles, use a ruler and water- or air-erasable pen to mark off the six 2½" x 4½" rectangles on the strip. Mark the rectangles approximately 1" apart to take full advantage of the color changes. As you cut rectangles from the strip, be sure to keep the lightest portion of each piece heading in the same direction, so that when you assemble the units the ombre effect is not lost.

## Making the Flying Geese Blocks

**1** Draw a diagonal line from corner to corner on the wrong side of the sand 2½" squares. Place one sand square on the end of an aqua 2½" x 4½" rectangle with right sides together. Stitch along the line. Trim the seam allowance ¼" from the stitching. Press the seam allowances away from the rectangle.

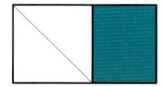 

**2** Stitch a sand 2½" square to the opposite end of the rectangle in the same manner to make a Flying Geese block that measures 2½" x 4½". Repeat

## Make it MARVELOUS
### from Vanessa Christenson

A designer by day, her sewing-superhero moniker is *Spinderella,* able to spin from one project to the next in a flash.

- **My latest marvelous binge is** chocolate.

- **If I had a three-word mantra, it would be** "Chocolate will help."

- **If I were a quilting superhero, my superpower in the sewing room would be** superfast speed, so I can move on to the next project and then the next!

- **One reason mini-quilts are fun to make:** You feel the success of completing a quilt top, quilting, and binding all in a day!

- **For general piecing, my go-to needle is** size 80/12.

- **On my mini playlist, what I'm listening to now is** whatever is playing on Pandora. I like top 40.

- **When making a mini-quilt, I'm more likely** to go to my scrap basket for fabric. Scrap all the way!

- **Here's a little tip on making it mini:** Make your binding smaller in width, so it's more proportionate to the quilt

with the taupe and pink rectangles. Make 18 total blocks—6 each of aqua, pink, and taupe.

Make 6 of each color.

## Assembling the Quilt Top

**1** Arrange the six aqua blocks in order from lightest to darkest. Sew the blocks together to make a vertical row; press the seam allowances in one direction. In the same manner, repeat to make a pink row and a taupe row.

**2** Lay out the three vertical rows, placing the middle row so that the flying geese point in the opposite direction of the outer rows. Join the rows; press the seam allowances in one direction.

Quilt assembly

## Finishing the Quilt

Go to ShopMartingale.com/HowtoQuilt for more details on quilting and finishing.

**1** Layer the backing, batting, and quilt top; baste the layers together. Hand or machine quilt as desired. The quilt shown was machine quilted with parallel vertical lines placed ¼" apart.

**2** Use the aqua 2"-wide strips to make the binding and attach it.

### Opposites are fun!

Which describes your current status better:

☐ **Streamlined Stash OR Supersized Stash** ☒

☐ **Press Seam Allowances Open OR Press to One Side** ☒

☐ **Salty OR Sweet** ☒

☒ **Steam OR No Steam** ☐

☐ **Prewashing OR No Prewashing** ☒

# A Pink Christmas

*Create an adorable miniature Christmas quilt in a pretty and unexpected pink palette. Wool and cotton appliqués combined with embroidery stitches lend a warm and cozy look to the snowy scene.*

Designed and made by Anne Sutton
**Finished size: 15" x 17"**

## Materials

*Cotton yardage is based on 42"-wide fabric. Fat quarters are 18" x 21" and fat eighths are 9" x 21".*

### Cotton

1 fat quarter of tan print for background

¼ yard of pink polka dot for borders

1 fat eighth of white print for hill

10" square of pink dot for bias vine

1 charm pack (or 10 to 15 squares, 5" x 5") or assorted scraps of pink, white, and brown prints for houses, trees, and gifts

⅛ yard of tan polka dot for corner squares

½ yard of pink stripe for binding

⅝ yard of fabric for backing

### Wool

1 rectangle, 4" x 6", of dark pink for truck, ornaments, and stars

1 rectangle, 4" x 6", of gray for stars, sheep face and legs, truck door and tires, arched door, and chimneys

1 rectangle, 2" x 5", of light pink for stars

1 square, 3" x 3", of medium pink for sheep and truck wheels

Scrap of white for heart and truck window

### Additional Materials

20" x 22" piece of batting

Freezer paper

Water-soluble fabric glue

Size 11 Sharp and size 24 chenille needles and 12-weight thread for wool appliqué and embroidery

## Cutting

*All measurements include ¼"-wide seam allowances.*

**From the tan print, cut:**
   1 rectangle, 12" x 14"

**From the white print, cut:**
   1 rectangle, 8" x 12"

**From the pink dot, cut:**
   1 bias strip, 1" x 9"

*Continued on page 43*

*Continued from page 41*

**From the pink polka dot, cut:**
2 rectangles, 2" x 14"
2 rectangles, 2" x 12"

**From the tan polka dot, cut:**
4 squares, 2" x 2"

**From the pink stripe, cut:**
2¼"-wide bias strips to total 80"

## Make it MARVELOUS
### from Anne Sutton

With her speedy appliqué skills and prolific pattern production, it may seem like Anne turns out twice as much as the average quilter. But it might be her superhero persona that deserves the kudos. Known as **The Multiplier**, her superhero side is able to simultaneously sew on two machines at once, turning a molehill of merry patchwork into a mountain in no time!

- **My latest marvelous binge is** watching *Downton Abbey*, the final season.

- **If I had a three-word mantra, it would be:** Have fun today.

- **If I were a quilting superhero, my superpower in the sewing room would be** the ability to sew on two machines simultaneously. I could get twice as much done!

- **One reason mini-quilts are fun to make:** They're so cute!

- **For general piecing, my go-to needle is** Microtex Sharp 70/10.

- **On my mini playlist, what I'm listening to now is** "I Believe in You" by Il Divo and Celine Dion, "Beautiful Day" by Lee Dewyze, and "Hello" by Adele.

- **When making a mini-quilt, I'm more likely** to go to my stash of uncut fabrics.

- **Here's a little tip on making it mini:** Use a mini (28mm) rotary cutter.

## Appliquéing the Quilt

1. Using your preferred appliqué method, prepare the hill for appliqué using the pattern on page 46 and the white 8" x 12" rectangle. Add a seam allowance along the top if you'll be turning the edge under. If you need more information, you can download free appliqué instructions at ShopMartingale.com/HowtoQuilt.

2. Place the hill on the tan background rectangle with right sides up, aligning the sides and lower edges. Pin or baste in place within the seam allowances, but leave the top edge open until the house and tree appliqués are added.

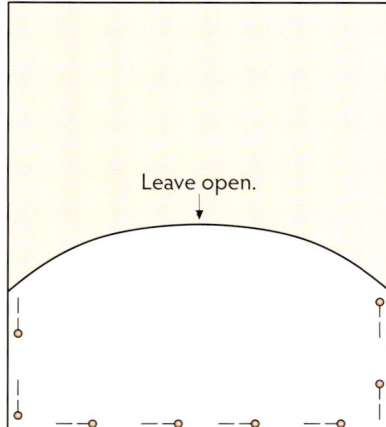

Leave open.

3. Prepare the remaining appliqué pieces from cotton and wool, referring to the materials list on page 41 and the patterns on page 45. In the quilt shown, the houses, trees, and gifts are cut from cotton prints and appliquéd using needle-turn appliqué. Prepare the wool appliqués by tracing the pattern pieces onto freezer paper. Cut out the patterns along the traced lines. Fuse the shiny side of the paper to the right side of the wool. Cut out the wool pieces following the paper edges. Remove the paper.

4. Make a bias vine using the pink 1" x 9" bias strip. Fold the strip wrong sides together and sew along the 9" edges using a ¼" seam allowance. Trim the seam allowance to ⅛" and press the strip so that the seam is centered on the back. Trim the strip to measure 8½" long.

**5** Referring to the photo on page 42 and the appliqué placement guide below, position the appliqué pieces on the background. Place the lower edges of the houses and tree trunks slightly beneath the top edge of the hill. Glue baste the wool appliqué pieces to the background. Pin or glue baste the cotton pieces in place. Appliqué the cotton pieces in place using your preferred method.

Appliqué placement guide

**6** Using 12-weight thread, blanket-stitch the edges of the wool appliqués. For details on the blanket stitch and other stitches, refer to "Embroidery Stiches" on page 79. Use a tiny stem stitch to embroider the windowpanes and gift ribbons. Use French knots to embroider the lamb's eyes and nose. Use a satin stitch to embroider the doorknobs.

## *Opposites are fun!*

Which describes your current status better:

☑ **Streamlined Stash OR Supersized Stash** ☐

☐ **Press Seam Allowances Open OR Press to One Side** ☑

☐ **Salty OR Sweet** ☑

☑ **Steam OR No Steam** ☐

☐ **Prewashing OR No Prewashing** ☑

## Assembling the Quilt Top

**1** Sew tan 2" squares to both ends of the pink polka-dot 2" x 12" strips. Press the seam allowances toward the strips.

**2** Sew the pink polka-dot 2" x 14" strips to the sides of the quilt center; press the seam allowances toward the strips. Sew the strips with tan squares to the top and bottom of the quilt; press the seam allowances toward the strips.

Quilt assembly

## Finishing the Quilt

Go to ShopMartingale.com/HowtoQuilt for more details on quilting and finishing.

**1** Layer the backing, batting, and quilt top; baste the layers together. Hand or machine quilt as desired. The quilt shown was machine quilted with various designs in the background to highlight the appliqués. The border was quilted with figure eights.

**2** Use the pink-striped 2¼"-wide bias strips to make the binding and attach it to the quilt.

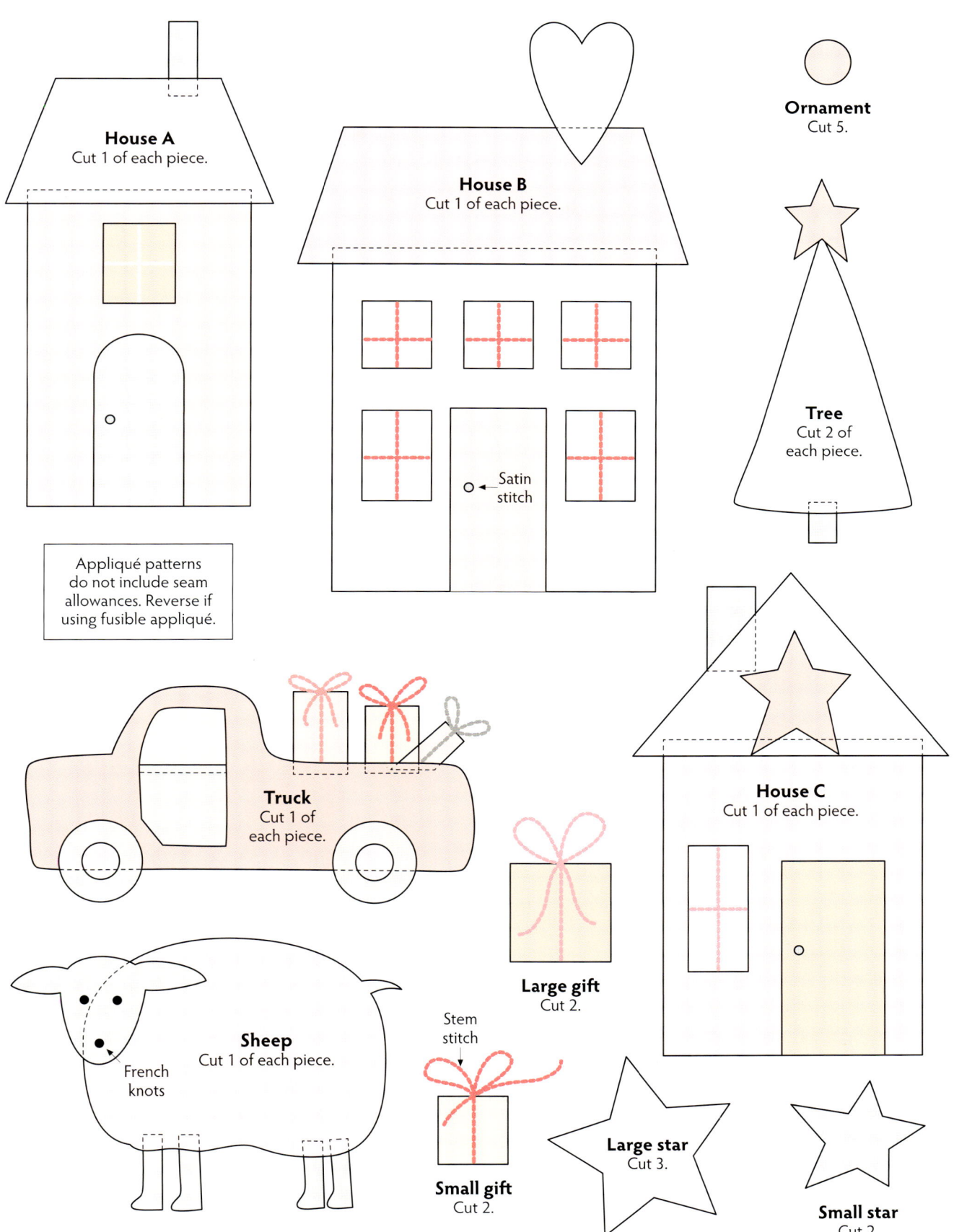

**House A**
Cut 1 of each piece.

**House B**
Cut 1 of each piece.

**Ornament**
Cut 5.

**Tree**
Cut 2 of
each piece.

Appliqué patterns
do not include seam
allowances. Reverse if
using fusible appliqué.

Satin
stitch

**Truck**
Cut 1 of
each piece.

**House C**
Cut 1 of each piece.

**Large gift**
Cut 2.

**Sheep**
Cut 1 of each piece.

French
knots

Stem
stitch

**Small gift**
Cut 2.

**Large star**
Cut 3.

**Small star**
Cut 2.

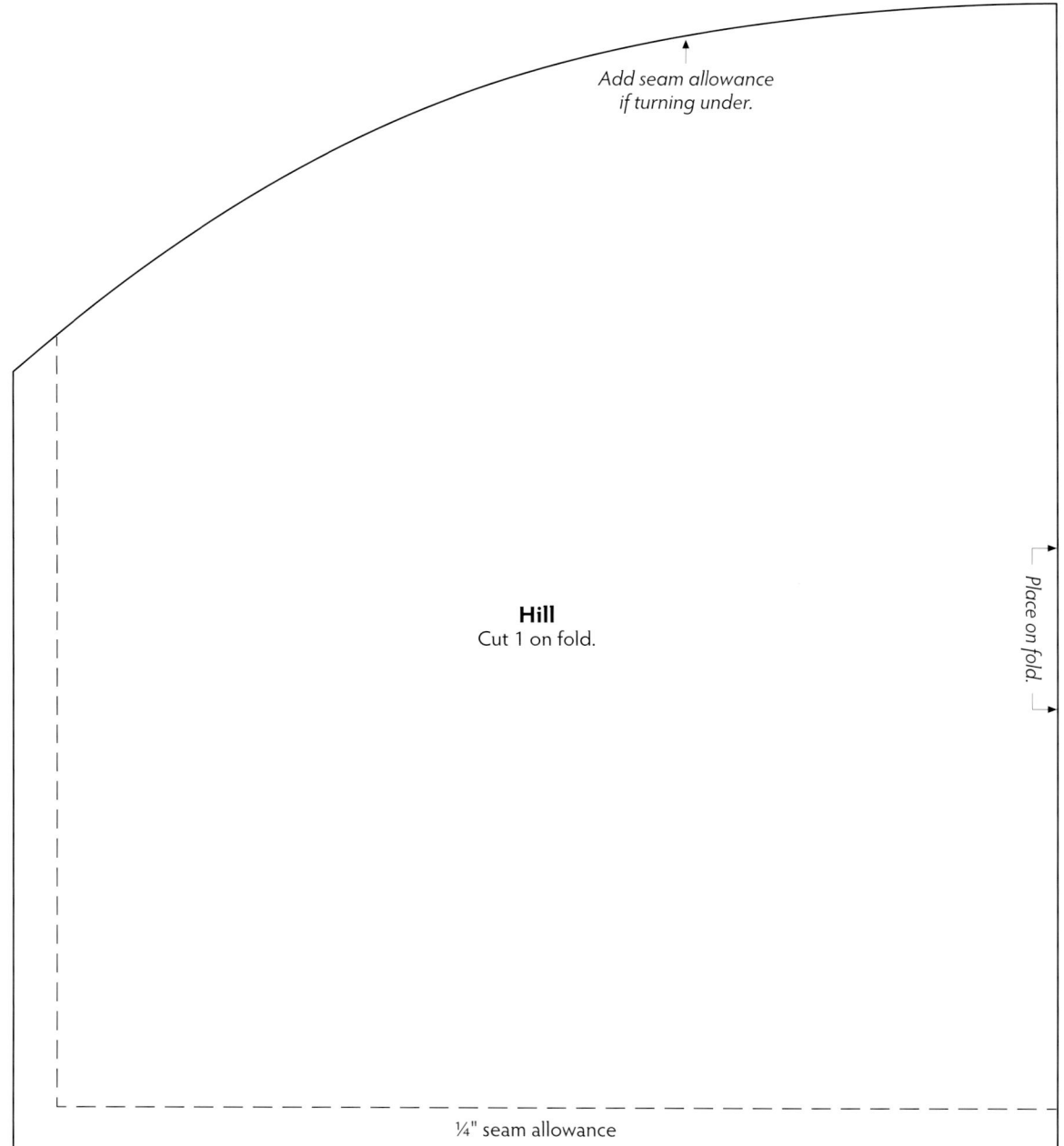

Add seam allowance
if turning under.

**Hill**
Cut 1 on fold.

Place on fold.

¼" seam allowance

# Spinner

*Swirling pinwheels spin around the outer edges of this bright and happy design. This mini makes a festive table topper for celebrating the arrival of spring, a birthday, or any other occasion.*

Designed and made by Me and My Sister Designs

**Finished size: 19½" x 19½"**

**Finished block: 5" x 5"**

## Materials

*Yardage is based on 42"-wide fabric.*

8 squares, 10" x 10", of assorted bright prints for blocks*

⅔ yard of white solid for blocks and sashing

¼ yard of multicolored diagonal stripe for binding

¾ yard of fabric for backing

25" x 25" piece of batting

*Precut Layer Cake squares work perfectly for this project.*

## Cutting

*All measurements include ¼"-wide seam allowances.*

**From *each* bright print, cut:**
- 4 rectangles, 1¾" x 3"
- 8 squares, 1¾" x 1¾"

**From the white solid, cut:**
- 2 strips, 3" x 42"; crosscut into 32 rectangles, 1¾" x 3"
- 2 strips, 1¾" x 42"; crosscut into 32 squares, 1¾" x 1¾"
- 2 strips, 1" x 42"; crosscut into 4 rectangles, 1" x 5½", and 4 rectangles, 1" x 6
- 2 strips, 2" x 42"; crosscut into 4 rectangles, 2" x 6", and 4 rectangles, 2" x 7½"
- 1 strip, 5½" x 42"; crosscut into 2 rectangles, 2½" x 5½", and 1 rectangle, 5½" x 9½"

**From the diagonal stripe, cut:**
- 3 strips, 2¼" x 42"

## Assembling the Blocks

Each Pinwheel block requires four matching bright 1¾" x 3" rectangles, eight matching bright 1¾" squares, four white 1¾" x 3" rectangles, and four white 1¾" squares.

**1** Draw a diagonal line from corner to corner on the wrong side of eight matching bright 1¾" squares. Place one bright square on the end of a white 1¾" x 3" rectangle with right sides together. Stitch along the line, and then trim the seam allowance to ¼". Press the resulting triangle open.

**2** Place a second square on the opposite end of the rectangle with right sides together. Sew and trim, and then press the triangle in the same manner as step 1. Make four flying-geese units that each measure 1¾" x 3".

 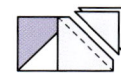 

Make 4.

**3** Draw a diagonal line from corner to corner on the wrong side of four white 1¾" squares. Place a white square on the left end of a matching print 1¾" x 3" rectangle with right sides together. Stitch along the line, and then trim the seam allowance to ¼". Press the triangle open, away from the rectangle. Make four units that each measure 1¾" x 3".

Make 4.

**4** Lay out the four flying-geese units and the units from step 3 as shown, forming a pinwheel design. Join each pair; press the seam allowances open. Join the four pairs; press the seam allowances open. The block should measure 5½" square. Repeat to make eight blocks.

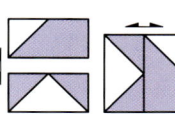 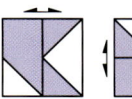 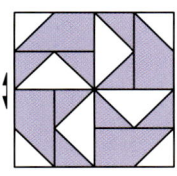

## Assembling the Quilt Top

**1** Select four blocks for the quilt corners, referring to the photo on page 47. For each of the corner blocks, sew a white 1" x 5½" strip to the right edge; press the seam allowances open. Sew a white 1" x 6" strip to the lower edge; press. Sew a 2" x 6" strip to the left edge; press. Sew a 2" x 7½" strip to the top edge; press. Repeat for each of the corner blocks. Each corner block should measure 7½" square.

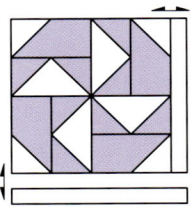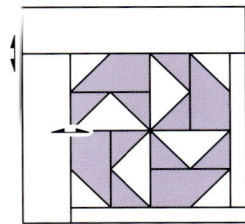

Make 4.

**2** Select two blocks for the center of the top and bottom of the quilt. Sew a white 2½" x 5½" rectangle to one edge of the block; press the seam allowances open. Make two that each measure 5½" x 7½".

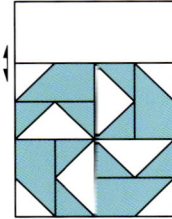

Make 2.

**3** Arrange the blocks in three rows as shown in the quilt assembly diagram, placing the 5½" x 9½" rectangle in the center. Join the blocks in each row; press the seam allowances open. Join the rows; press.

Quilt assembly

## Finishing the Quilt

Go to ShopMartingale.com/HowtoQuilt for more details on quilting and finishing.

**1** Layer the backing, batting, and quilt top; baste the layers together. Hand or machine quilt as desired. The quilt shown was machine quilted with an allover design of swirling loops.

**2** Use the striped 2¼"-wide strips to make the binding and attach it to the quilt.

## Opposites are fun!

Which describes your current status better:

[X] **Streamlined Stash OR Supersized Stash** [ ]

[X] **Press Seam Allowances Open OR Press to One Side** [ ]

Barb [X] **Salty OR Sweet** [X] Mary

[X] **Steam OR No Steam** [ ]

[ ] **Prewashing OR No Prewashing** [X]

# Stars and Stars

## Materials

*Yardage is based on 42"-wide fabric. Scrap sizes are approximate.*

⅓ yard of red print for borders and binding

16 scraps, 3" x 15", of assorted light prints for blocks

10 scraps, 4" x 12", of assorted blue prints for blocks

6 scraps, 4" x 12", of assorted red prints for blocks

⅝ yard of fabric for backing

22" x 22" piece of batting

## Cutting

*All measurements include ¼"-wide seam allowances. The pieces cut from scraps are oversized for paper piecing and don't need to be cut precisely.*

**From *each* red or blue scrap, cut:**
   3 rectangles, 2" x 2½"
   1 square, 3½" x 3½"

**From *each* light print, cut**
   4 squares, 2½" x 2½"
   1 rectangle, 2½" x 3"

**From the red print, cut:**
   2 strips, 3" x 17½"
   2 strips, 3" x 12½"
   2 strips, 2" x 42"

*Combine red, white, and blue prints with little stars for a charming and patriotic mini-quilt. Paper piece the star blocks for speed and precision.*

Designed and made by Laurie Simpson
**Finished size:** 17½" x 17½"
**Finished block:** 3" x 3"

She may seem like a shy get-along gal by day, but the **Quantum Quarter-Master** superhero within is able to command the perfect ¼" seam at all times and in all places. Her perfect piecing powers draw attention every time. Ten-hut!

- **My latest marvelous binge is** watching "A Place to Call Home," an Australian soap opera, and "Occupied," a Norwegian political drama.

- **If I had a three-word mantra, it would be:** Three-run homer!

- **If I were a quilting superhero, my superpower in the sewing room would be** accurate machine piecing. I have a long, long way to go.

- **One reason mini-quilts are fun to make:** You can quickly finish one and make another!

- **For general piecing, my go-to needle is** a Universal.

- **On my mini playlist, what I'm listening to now is** "Bewitched, Bothered and Bewildered" by Ella Fitzgerald, "Misty" by Sarah Vaughan, and "Wave" by Sarah Vaughan.

- **When making a mini-quilt, I'm more likely** to go to my scrap basket for fabric. Always scraps!

- **Here's a little tip on making it mini:** Remember to enjoy it!

## Assembling the Blocks

For more information on paper piecing, visit ShopMartingale.com/HowtoQuilt to download free instructions.

1 Make 16 copies each of paper-piecing patterns A, B, and C on page 55.

2 Beginning with pattern piece A, place a blue 2" x 2½" rectangle over the space marked 1. The fabric should be right side up on the unprinted side of the pattern. Hold the paper up to the light to make sure that the entire space is covered.

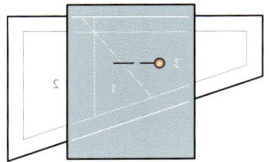

3 Place a light 2½" square right sides together with the blue print, aligning raw edges and making sure that there is ¼" beyond the line between space 1 and 2. Pin the pieces to the paper.

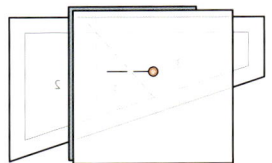

4 Turn the pattern to the printed side and sew on the line between space 1 and 2 using a very short stitch length. This will perforate the paper, making it easier to remove later.

5 Trim the seam allowance (only the fabric, not the paper!) to ¼" if needed and press. After pressing, trim the blue piece ¼" beyond the line that separates sections 1 and 3, to prepare for adding the next piece of fabric.

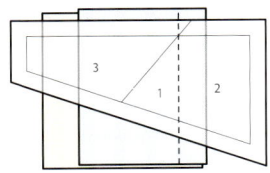

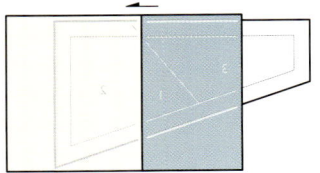

**6** Place a matching light 2½" x 3" rectangle right sides together with piece 1, covering the line between spaces 1 and 3. Pin, sew on the line between 1 and 3, trim, and press as before.

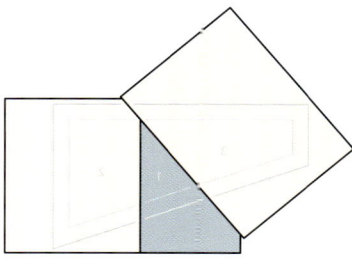

**7** Trim the edges of the unit even with the outer dashed lines of the pattern to complete unit A.

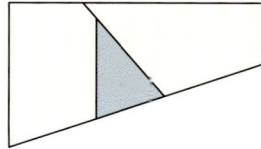

**8** Piece unit B in a similar manner, using a matching blue 2" x 2½" rectangle for space 1, a light 2½" square for space 2, and a blue 3½" square for space 3.

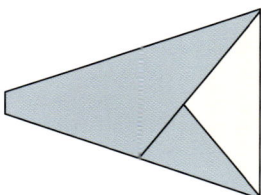

**9** Piece unit C using a matching blue 2" x 2½" rectangle for space 1 and two matching light 2½" squares for spaces 2 and 3.

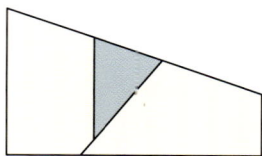

**10** Join the three units, sewing through the paper along the lines to complete the block. Each Star block should measure 3½" square. Press the seam allowances in one direction or open. Leave the paper on until the blocks are joined together to make the quilt center.

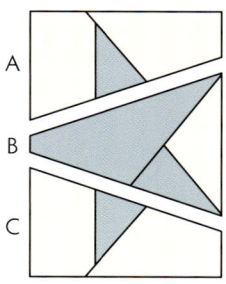
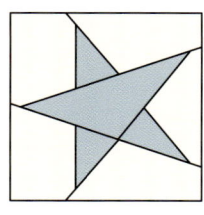

**11** Repeat steps 2–10 to make ten blue and six red blocks.

## Assembling the Quilt Top

**1** Arrange the blocks in four rows of four as shown. Join the blocks in each row; press the seam allowances in opposite directions from row to row. Join the rows; press the seam allowance in one direction.

**2** Gently remove the paper from the blocks.

**3** Sew the red 3" x 12½" strips to the sides of the quilt center. Press the seam allowances toward the strips. Sew the red 3" x 17½" strips to the top and bottom of the quilt; press.

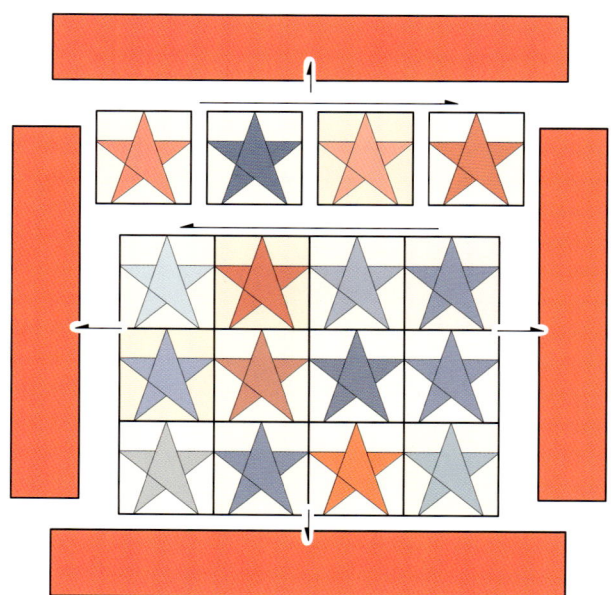

Quilt assembly

## Finishing the Quilt

Go to ShopMartingale.com/HowtoQuilt for more details on quilting and finishing.

1 Layer the backing, batting, and quilt top; baste the layers together. Hand or machine quilt as desired. The quilt shown was hand quilted with a hanging diamond design in the blocks and a fan design in the border.

2 Use the red 2"-wide strips to make the binding and attach it.

### Opposites are fun!

Which describes your current status better:

☐ **Streamlined Stash OR Supersized Stash** ▨

▨ **Press Seam Allowances Open OR Press to One Side** ☐

☐ **Salty OR Sweet** ▨

▨ **Steam OR No Steam** ☐

☐ **Prewashing OR No Prewashing** ▨

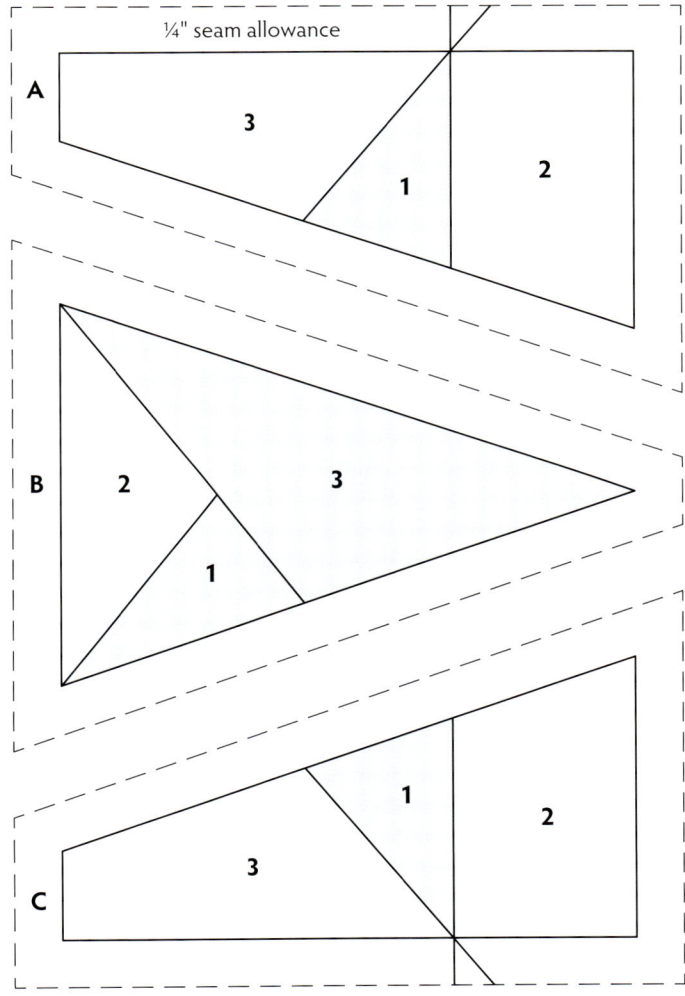

¼" seam allowance

A — 3, 1, 2

B — 2, 1, 3

C — 3, 1, 2

# June Bug

This charming mini features simple strip-pieced blocks and orange-peel appliqués. You'll save time by using precut 5" squares for the blocks.

Designed and made by Camille Roskelley

**Finished size:** 15½" x 15½"

**Finished block:** 4" x 4"

## Materials

*Fat quarters measure approximately 18" x 21".*

11 squares, 5" x 5", of assorted prints for blocks*

1 fat quarter of white solid for blocks

1 fat quarter of aqua print for border

1 fat quarter of diagonal stripe for binding

1 fat quarter of fabric for backing**

18" x 18" piece of batting

⅓ yard of 18"-wide lightweight fusible web

*Precut charm squares work perfectly for this project.*

**As an alternative, Camille suggests using 16 charm squares (5" x 5") to make a pieced backing.*

## Cutting

*All measurements include ¼"-wide seam allowances.*

**From the white solid, cut:**
  5 squares, 4½" x 4½"

**From 6 of the assorted-print squares, cut a *total* of:**
  16 strips, 1½" x 4½"

**From the aqua print, cut:**
  2 strips, 2" x 12½"
  2 strips, 2" x 15½"

**From the diagonal stripe, cut:**
  4 strips, 2" x 21"

## Make it MARVELOUS
### from Camille Roskelley

It's all thimbles and blossoms for Camille until she puts her sewing skills into hyperdrive as her superhero self, the **Whirling Dervish,** able to do double-time on whatever project she has in progress.

- **My latest marvelous binge is** watching *Gilmore Girls.*

- **If I had a three-word mantra, it would be:** Keep it simple.

- **If I were a quilting superhero, my superpower in the sewing room would be** superspeed. I'd finally making a dent in my quilting bucket list.

- **One reason mini-quilts are fun to make:** You can display a whole bunch of them in your sewing room alltogether—the more the better. I need more walls....

- **For general piecing, my go-to needle is** size 80/12 Universal. I buy them by the box.

- **On my mini playlist, what I'm listening to now is** "Sugar" by Maroon 5, "Sweet Disposition" by The Temper Trap, and "Where Does the Good Go" by Tegan and Sara.

- **When making a mini-quilt, I'm more likely** to go to my scrap basket, all the way!

- **Here's a little tip on making it mini:** Think little. Little prints work best.

## Assembling the Blocks

**1** Trace the complete pattern for the orange peel (four petals and outside square) on page 59 onto the paper side of fusible web. Make five traced patterns and cut them out on the lines of the square.

**2** Following the manufacturer's instructions, fuse one square to the wrong side of each of the five uncut 5" squares, centering the fusible web on the fabric square. Cut each petal out along the lines, leaving the rest of the fused square intact. Remove the paper backing and set aside.

**3** Arrange four matching petals on a white 4½" square using the fusible-web paper from step 2 as a guide for placement. Fuse the petals in place and blanket-stitch the edge of each petal by hand or machine. If you need more information, you can download free appliqué instructions at ShopMartingale.com/HowtoQuilt. For details on the hand blanket stitch, refer to "Embroidery Stitches" on page 79. Make five appliquéd blocks.

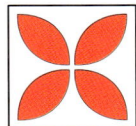

Make 5.

**4** Sew four assorted print 1½" x 4½" strips together to make a block measuring 4½" square. Press the seam allowances in one direction. Make four pieced blocks.

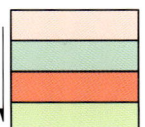

Make 4 .

## Assembling the Quilt Top

**1** Lay out three rows of three blocks each, alternating the blocks as shown. Join the blocks in each row; press the seam allowances open. Join the rows; press the seam allowances open.

**2** Sew the aqua 2" x 12½" strips to the sides of the quilt; press the seam allowances toward the border. Sew the aqua 2" x 15½" strips to the top and bottom of the quilt and press.

## Finishing the Quilt

Go to ShopMartingale.com/HowtoQuilt for more details on quilting and finishing.

**1** Layer the backing, batting, and quilt top; baste the layers together. Hand or machine quilt as desired. The quilt shown was machine quilted with parallel straight lines.

**2** Use the striped 2"-wide strips to make the binding and attach it to the quilt.

Quilt assembly

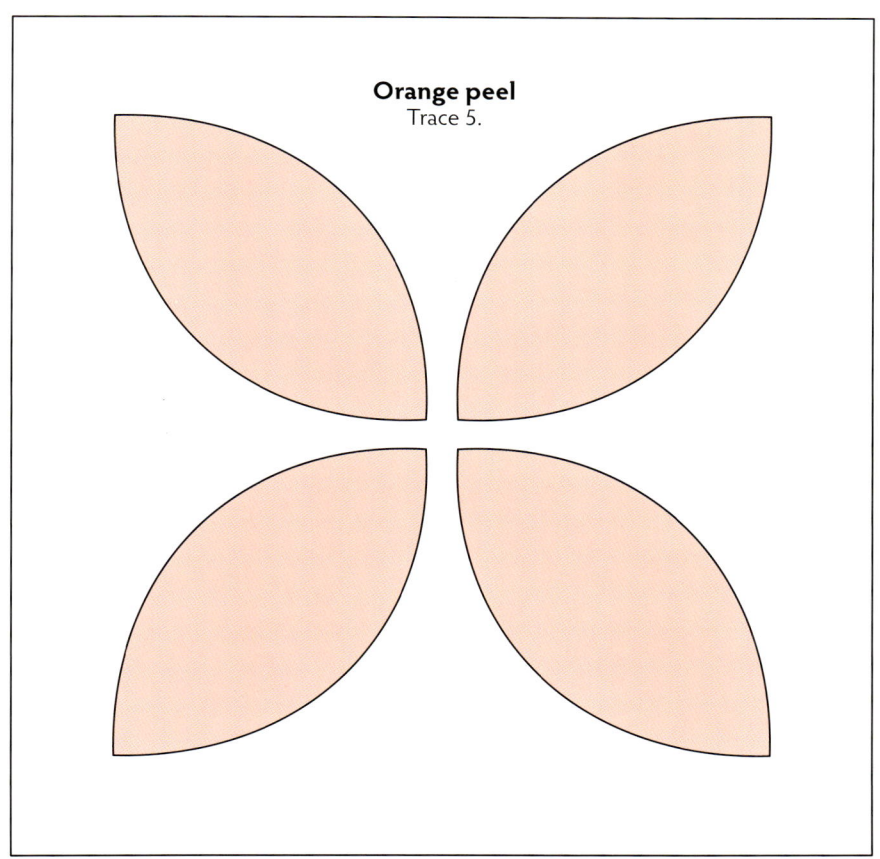

**Orange peel**
Trace 5.

Appliqué patterns do not include seam allowances.

# Fly Away Home

This bright and colorful quilt is fun to stitch using a clever quilt-as-you-go technique to piece the random, raw-edge Log Cabin blocks. A graceful swallow appliqué adds the perfect finishing touch.

Designed and made by Jen Kingwell
**Finished size:** 13" x 13"

## Materials

*Yardage is based on 42"-wide fabrics.*

½ yard *total* of assorted print scraps, 1½" to 2" wide, for raw-edge piecing and binding

5" x 5" square of black print for bird appliqué

1 fat quarter of fabric for backing

15" x 15" piece of batting

Water-soluble fabric glue

Fabric marking pen that will show up on batting

12-weight thread in assorted colors for hand quilting

## Cutting

*All measurements include ¼"-wide seam allowances. Note that Jen tore the 1½"-wide strips for a ragged raw-edge look.*

**From the backing fabric, cut:**
1 square, 15" x 15"

**From the assorted print scraps, cut:**
4 squares, 1½" x 1½"
Approximately 60 strips, 1½" wide x varying lengths from 2" to 7"
2"-wide strips to total 60"

## Make it MARVELOUS
from Jen Kingwell

It hardly seems fair that Australian designer Jen, whose local time is perpetually 16 hours ahead of the nearest US time zone, could get the jump on what's ahead for all of us. But in fact, her superhero side is able to do just that! As **Futurama Mama,** she's able to see well into the future. She's been there and done that before the rest of us are even up and out of bed!

- **My latest marvelous binge is** listening to season one of the podcast *Serial.* (Yay, I have season two still to go!)

- **If I had a three-word mantra, it would be:** Live life large. Or, Gerard Butler rules. Or, It'll quilt out.

- **If I were a quilting superhero, my superpower in the sewing room would be** the ability to see into the future. Then I could (and would) be more organized.

- **One reason mini-quilts are fun to make:** I like little piecing, so minis are just an excuse for even smaller pieces.

- **For general piecing, my go-to needle is** size 11 Straw for hand piecing.

- **On my mini playlist, what I'm listening to now is** "Video Games" by Lana Del Rey, "Hello" by Adele, and "Gravity" by Sara Bareilles.

- **When making a mini-quilt, I'm more likely** to go to my stash of uncut fabrics.

- **Here's a little tip on making it mini:** Use as many fabrics as you can possibly squeeze in!

## Assembling the Quilt Top

**1** Draw a 13" square on the batting, centering it. Divide the square in half vertically and horizontally to create four quadrants.

**2** Center the batting on the wrong side of the 15" square of backing fabric; pin or baste the edges. In one quadrant, place a print 1½" square right side up near the center. Use a dab of fabric glue to hold it in place; then stitch parallel lines through all layers to secure the square. Jen quilted by hand using a running stitch (see "Embroidery Stitches" on page 79), but you could also stitch by machine.

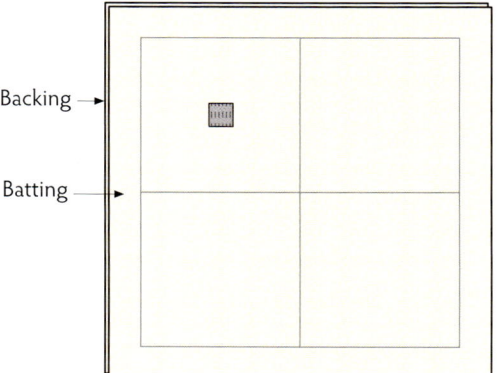

**3** Place a print strip along the right edge of the square. Overlap the edges slightly and trim the end of the strips so that it's slightly longer than the square; secure with a dab of glue and stitch in place. Leave the edges of the pieces raw.

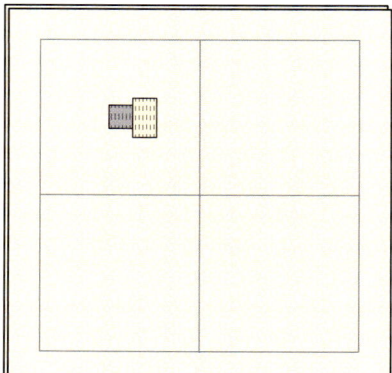

**4** Continue adding strips around the square in an improvisational manner (don't worry about them all being straight and parallel!), creating a Log Cabin block. Trim the strips as needed to fit. You can vary the widths of the strips if desired.

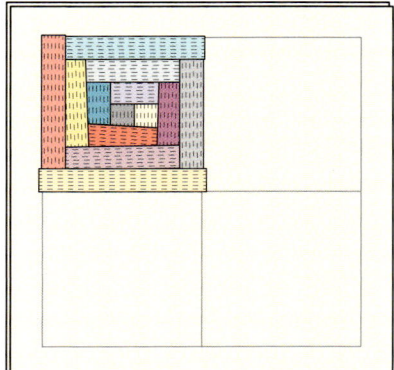

**5** Repeat steps 2–4 to cover each quadrant with strips, mixing strip colors and lengths as desired.

**6** Using the swallow pattern, right, and the black 5" square, prepare the swallow for your preferred method of appliqué. Jen used needle-turn appliqué. If you prefer to use fusible appliqué, you will need to reverse the pattern first. If you need more information, you can download free appliqué instructions at ShopMartingale.com/HowtoQuilt. Place the swallow in the upper-right quadrant and appliqué in place.

## Finishing the Quilt

Go to ShopMartingale.com/HowtoQuilt for more details on finishing.

**1** Trim the excess batting and backing fabric even with the edges of the quilt top.

**2** Join the 2"-wide strips end to end to make approximately 60" of binding; attach the binding to the quilt.

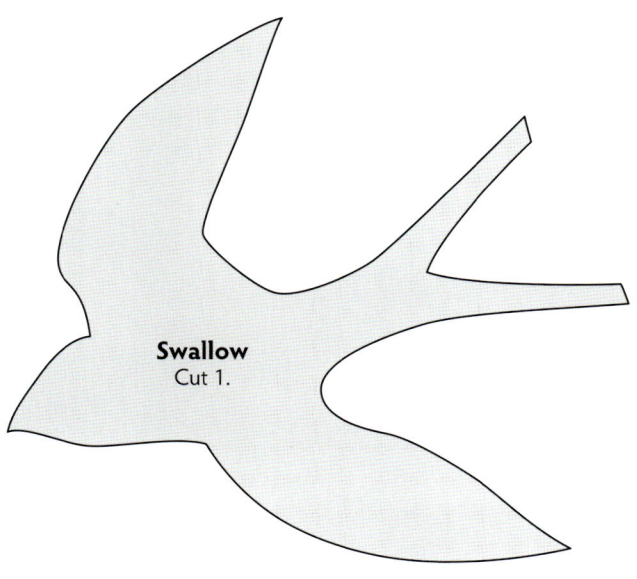

**Swallow**
Cut 1.

Appliqué pattern does not include seam allowances. Reverse if using fusible appliqué.

## Opposites *are fun!*

Which describes your current status better:

- ☐ Streamlined Stash OR Supersized Stash ☒
- ☐ Press Seam Allowances Open OR Press to One Side ☒
- ☒ Salty OR Sweet ☐
- ☒ Steam OR No Steam ☐
- ☐ Prewashing OR No Prewashing ☒

# Midnight Garden

Make a beautiful mini-quilt adorned with wool appliqués of swirling vines and flowers. Finish your garden with hand embroidery in lovely pearl cotton threads for gorgeous texture and dimension.

Designed and made by Lisa Bongean
**Finished size:** 17½" x 17½"

## Materials

*Cotton yardage is based on 42"-wide fabrics. Fat quarters measure approximately 18" x 21".*

### Cotton

⅝ yard of black solid for background, borders, and binding

1 fat quarter of green print for triangle border

⅝ yard of fabric for backing

### Wool

1 rectangle, 6" x 8", of sage for leaves

1 rectangle, 4" x 9", of green for stems and vines

1 rectangle, 4" x 8", of red tweed for large, medium, and small flowers

9 rectangles, 4" x 5" *each*, of assorted colors (bright red, rust red, purple, teal, light blue, periwinkle, orange, pink, and yellow) for flowers

Assorted scraps of gold, cream, and chocolate for flower centers

Assorted scraps of green for leaves

### Additional Materials

22" x 22" piece of batting

¾ yard of 18"-wide lightweight fusible web

White marking pen (such as Clover brand)

Size 24 Chenille needle and pearl cotton in coordinating colors*

½"-finished half-square-triangle piecing paper (such as Primitive Gatherings Triangle Paper; optional)

*Lisa used #12 Valdani pearl cotton in the following colors: M81, P9, 078, H212, P11, 0154, 1, 0178, P12*

## Cutting

*All measurements include ¼"-wide seam allowances.*

**From the black solid, cut:**
  1 square, 11" x 11"
  1 rectangle, 8½" x 11½" OR 42 squares, 1⅜" x 1⅜"*
  2 rectangles, 3½" x 17½"
  2 rectangles, 3½" x 11½"
  2 binding strips, 2" x 42"

**From the green print, cut:**
  1 rectangle, 8½" x 11½" OR 42 squares, 1⅜" x 1⅜"*

*If you use Primitive Gatherings Triangle Paper, cut the large rectangles; if you'll be piecing units traditionally, cut the small squares.*

## Make it MARVELOUS
### from Lisa Bongean

Some say it takes a village, but designer Lisa simply needs a case of cans for her superhero side to get the job done—spray-starch cans, that is. As the superhero **Starch Madness,** she gets her patchwork pieces precisely put together with nary a slip!

- **My latest marvelous binge is** buying a new house!

- **If I had a three-word mantra, it would be:** Make it fun.

- **If I were a quilting superhero, my superpower in the sewing room would be** seeing the future so I would know whether people will like my latest fabric and quilt designs.

- **One reason mini-quilts are fun to make:** They are like babies—just irresistible!

- **For general piecing, my go-to needle is** size 75/11.

- **On my mini playlist, what I'm listening to now is** "Mr. Misunderstood" by Eric Church, "Hello" by Adele, and "Don't Stop Believin'" by Journey.

- **When making a mini-quilt, I'm more likely** to go to my stash of uncut fabrics, because I'll have to kit it!

- **Here's a little tip on making it mini:** Starch your fabrics first thing. (See "Starch for Stability" on page 6.)

## Preparing the Appliqués

1 Referring to the patterns on page 69, trace the flowers and leaves onto fusible web. To save time, Lisa recommends cutting a piece of fusible web the same size as each wool rectangle. Then trace as many flowers or leaves on each as you can fit, making sure you'll have the total number of each piece called for. Make sure to trace the large center flower onto the 4" x 8" fusible web piece and fuse it to the red tweed. Fuse the leaves to the sage wool and assorted green wool scraps. Fuse the flower centers to assorted wool scraps, following the manufacturer's instructions. Refer to the materials list and project photo for color ideas.

2 Cut out the shapes on the drawn lines and remove the paper from the fusible web. For more information, download free wool-appliqué instructions at ShopMartingale.com/HowtoQuilt.

3 For the stems in the center square, cut a 1" x 8½" piece of fusible web. Fuse it to the green wool 4" x 9" rectangle. Cut out the strip. With a rotary cutter and ruler, cut it into two strips, ³⁄₁₆" wide, for the straight stems, and four strips, ⅛" wide, for the curved stems. Cut each strip in half so that you have four strips, ³⁄₁₆" x 4¼", and eight strips, ⅛" x 4¼". Carefully remove the backing paper.

4 For the border vines, fuse a 2" x 8½" fusible web strip onto the remaining green wool. Cut the strip into eight strips, ³⁄₁₆" wide. Remove the backing paper.

## Appliquéing the Center

1 Place the large center flower, four medium flowers, eight small flowers, the stems, and the leaves right side up on the black 11" square according to the placement diagram below. The slight tackiness of the fusible web will help keep the pieces in place. The shapes should slightly overlap as needed rather than butting up against each other. Fuse the shapes, using generous steam and moving the iron constantly to avoid scorching the wool.

Appliqué placement guide

2 Blanket-stitch the perimeter of each flower and leaf with coordinating pearl cotton thread. Cross-stitch over the stems. For details on hand-embroidery stitches, see "Embroidery Stitches" on page 79.

**3** Using the white marking pen, draw eight curved lines and a circle in the middle of the center flower as shown. Embroider on the curved drawn lines using a feather stitch. Stitch a circle of French knots in the flower center and add them to the ends of the feather stitches.

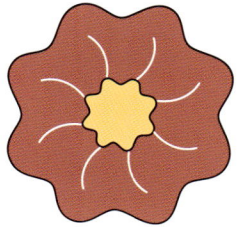 

Large center flower

**4** For the small flowers, embroider long blanket stitches in the indents of the flower petals. Stitch a French knot in the center.

Small flowers

**5** For the medium flowers, stitch long blanket stitches around the center circle. Stitch a French knot at the flower center.

Medium flowers

**6** Trim the center to 10½" x 10½".

## Assembling the Sawtooth Border

Lisa recommends triangle piecing paper because the half-square-triangle units for the border finish at just ½". She uses Primitive Gatherings triangle piecing paper; one sheet yields 84 half-square-triangle units, the exact number needed. As an alternative, you can make the units two at a time starting with 1⅜" squares. See "Half-Square-Triangle Pairs," above right.

**1** Align the black and green 8½" x 11½" rectangles, right sides together. Place one sheet of triangle piecing paper over the fabric.

---

### Half-Square-Triangle Pairs

**1** Draw a line from corner to corner on the wrong side of the green 1⅜" squares.

**2** Layer a marked green square right sides together with a black 1⅜" square. Sew ¼" from each side of the line. Cut along the drawn line and press the seam allowances toward the black triangles. Make a total of 84 half-square-triangle units. Each unit should be 1" square.

Make 84.

**2** Follow the manufacturer's instructions to sew, cut, press, and trim the half-square-triangle units. Each individual unit should be 1" square.

Make 84.

**3** Join 20 units for the side borders, making sure to orient the triangles as shown. Make two. Each border should measure 1" x 10½".

Make 2.

**4** Join 22 units as shown for the top and bottom borders, making sure to orient the triangles correctly. Make two. Each border should measure 1" x 11½".

Make 2.

**5** Sew the side borders to the sides of the center square; press the seam allowances toward the square. Sew the top and bottom borders to the center square; press.

## Adding the Appliqué Border

**1** Sew the black 3½" x 11½" rectangles to the sides of the quilt center; press toward the rectangles. Sew the 3½" x 17½" rectangles to the top and bottom of the quilt center; press.

**2** Use a white chalk pen to trace the curved vine shapes onto the borders. Place each ³⁄₁₆"-wide vine along the white lines, gently finger-pressing in place. Fuse the vines.

**3** Add the remaining prepared appliqués according to the placement diagram. You should have eight medium flowers, 41 small flowers, and 42 small leaves. Blanket-stitch the edges of all flowers and leaves. Cross-stitch over the vines. Embroider a French knot in the middle of each medium and small flower.

**4** Using the white chalk, draw curved stems from the vine to the flowers as desired. Embroider the stems with a stem stitch.

## Finishing the Quilt

Go to ShopMartingale.com/HowtoQuilt for more details on quilting and finishing.

**1** Layer the backing, batting, and quilt top; baste the layers together. Hand or machine quilt as desired.

**2** Use the black 2"-wide strips to make the binding and attach it to the quilt.

*Opposites are fun!*

Which describes your current status better:

☐ **Streamlined Stash OR Supersized Stash** ▨

▨ **Press Seam Allowances Open OR Press to One Side** ☐

☐ **Salty OR Sweet** ▨

▨ **Steam OR No Steam** ☐

☐ **Prewashing OR No Prewashing** ▨
(Starch instead of water.)

Appliqué placement

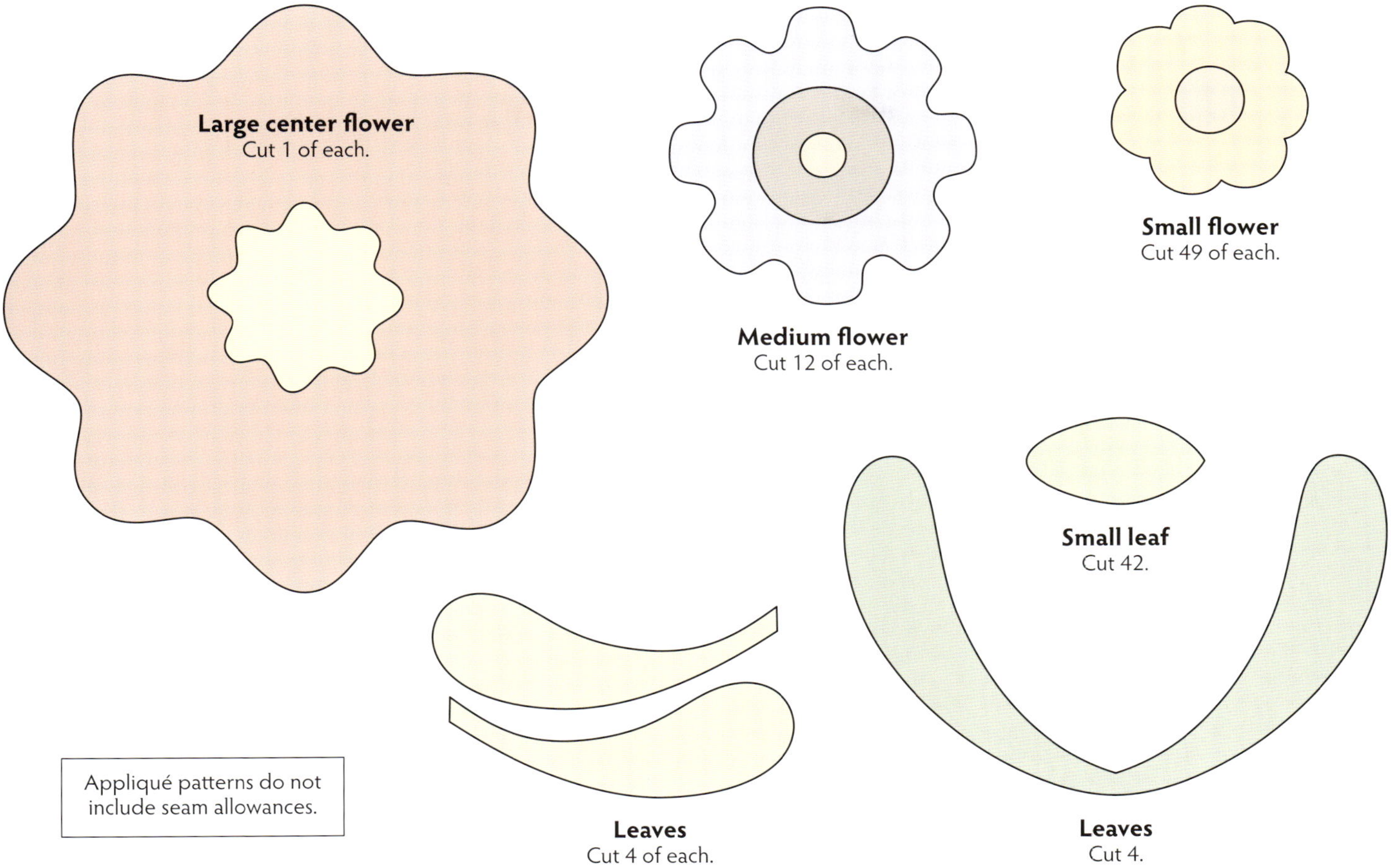

**Large center flower**
Cut 1 of each.

**Medium flower**
Cut 12 of each.

**Small flower**
Cut 49 of each.

**Small leaf**
Cut 42.

Appliqué patterns do not include seam allowances.

**Leaves**
Cut 4 of each.

**Leaves**
Cut 4.

# Mini Medallion

*The timeless combination of blue, cream, and brown create an elegant medallion quilt featuring a Sawtooth Star block surrounded by flying-geese and broken-dishes borders.*

Designed and made by Betsy Chutchian
**Finished size:** 17½" x 17½"

## Materials

*Yardage is based on 42"-wide fabrics. Fat eighths measure approximately 9" x 21".*

½ yard of indigo floral for star block, broken-dishes border, and outer border

¼ yard *total* of assorted beige prints for block and broken-dishes border

¼ yard *total* of assorted brown and slate-blue prints for broken-dishes border

¼ yard of cream solid for outer border

⅛ yard or 1 fat eighth of blue floral for flying-geese border

1 fat eighth of brown floral for flying-geese border

¼ yard of brown check for binding

⅝ yard of fabric for backing

22" x 22" piece of batting

1"-finished half-square-triangle papers (such as Spinning Star Designs Star Singles; optional)

## Cutting

*All measurements include ¼"-wide seam allowances.*

**From *1 of the beige prints*, cut:**
  1 square, 3¼" x 3¼"
  4 squares, 1½" x 1½"

**From the remaining assorted beige prints, cut:**\*
  40 squares, 2" x 2", OR 10 squares, 4½" x 4½"

**From the indigo floral, cut:**
  4 strips, 2½" x 42"; crosscut into 53 squares, 2½" x 2½"
  4 squares, 3" x 3"
  4 squares, 1⅞" x 1⅞"

**From the brown floral, cut:**
  24 squares, 1⅞" x 1⅞"

**From the blue floral, cut:**
  6 squares, 3¼" x 3¼"

**From the assorted brown and blue prints (including the indigo floral), cut a *total* of:**
  40 squares, 2" x 2", OR 10 squares, 4½" x 4½"

*\*If you're using Star Singles half-square-triangle papers, cut the 4½" squares and follow the manufacturer's instructions. You'll need to make 80 half-square-triangle units.*

*Continued on page 72*

*Continued from page 70*

**From the cream solid, cut:**
2 strips, 3" x 42"; crosscut into:
4 squares, 3" x 3"
24 rectangles, 2½" x 3"

**From the brown check, cut:**\*\*
2 strips, 1⅛" x 42"

\*\**These strips are for single-fold binding. Cut 2 strips, 2" x 42", for double-fold binding.*

## Assembling the Sawtooth Star Block

**1** Draw a diagonal line from corner to corner on the wrong sides of the indigo 1⅞" squares. Place two marked squares with right sides together on opposite corners of the beige print 3¼" square as shown, matching the drawn lines. Sew a scant ¼" from each side of the drawn line.

**2** Cut the unit along the drawn line to yield two units. Press the seam allowances toward the indigo triangles.

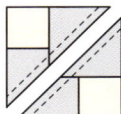 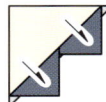

**3** Place a marked indigo square with right sides together on the corner of the pressed unit, orienting the line as shown. Sew a scant ¼" from each side of the line. Cut along the drawn line to yield two flying-geese units. Press the seam allowances toward the indigo print. Make four indigo/cream flying-geese units. Each unit should measure 1½" x 2½".

 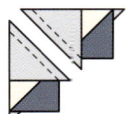 

Make 4.

### Make it MARVELOUS
#### from Betsy Chutchian

***Captain Cleaner Upper*** is the guise under which Betsy hangs her superhero star. The younger sibling of ***Neat Freakly,*** she'll sequentially sort your scraps before your rotary cutter is closed!

- **My latest marvelous binge is** watching *Grace and Frankie* on Netflix.
- **If I had a three-word mantra, it would be:** More is better.
- **If I were a quilting superhero, my superpower in the sewing room would be** a neat-freak ability to clean up what I cut up.
- **One reason mini-quilts are fun to make:** You can make the same blocks and settings used in large quilts, but in a much shorter amount of time.
- **For general piecing, my go-to needle is** a Microtex 80/12.
- **On my mini playlist, what I'm listening to now is** "Hello" and anything else Adele sings.
- **When making a mini-quilt, I'm more likely** to go to both my scrap basket and to my stash of uncut fabrics. I prefer to use leftovers from other projects that are already on the cutting table.
- **Here's a little tip on making it mini:** Cut oversized pieces, sew together, and then trim to the size needed.

**4** Lay out the four flying-geese units with the four matching beige 1½" squares and one indigo 2½" square in three rows. Join the units in each row; press the seam allowances open. Join the rows; press. The Sawtooth Star should measure 4½" square.

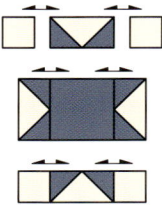 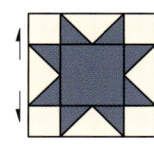

## Assembling the Flying-Geese Border

**1** Draw a diagonal line from corner to corner on the wrong sides of the brown-floral 1⅞" squares. Place two marked squares with right sides together on opposite corners of the blue-floral 3¼" square. Repeat steps 1–3 of "Assembling the Sawtooth Star Block" on page 72 to make four flying-geese units. Make 24 total. Each unit should measure 1½" x 2½".

Make 24.

**2** Join four flying-geese units along the long edges as shown. Press the seam allowances in one direction. Make two. Each strip should measure 2½" x 4½".

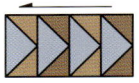

Make 2 .

**3** Sew six flying-geese units together along the long edges; press. Sew two flying-geese units together, and then sew them to one end as shown; press. Make two. Each strip should measure 2½" x 8½".

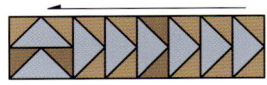

Make 2 .

**4** Sew the strips of four flying-geese units to opposite sides of the Sawtooth Star block; press the seam allowances as shown or press them open to minimize bulk. Sew the strips of eight flying-geese units to the top and bottom and press. The piece should be 8½" square.

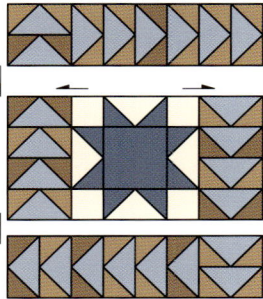

## Assembling the Broken-Dishes Border

If you're using purchased half-square-triangle papers, follow the manufacturer's instructions to make eighty 1"-finished half-square-triangle units from the beige print and assorted blue and brown prints. Follow the instructions below if you're not using the papers.

**1** Draw a diagonal line from corner to corner on the wrong side of the beige 2" squares. Place a beige square right sides together with a blue or brown 2" square. Stitch ¼" from each side of the drawn line. Cut along the line to yield two half-square-triangle units. Press the seam allowances toward the dark fabric. Trim each unit to 1½" square. Make four units.

Make 4.

**2** Arrange four half-square-triangle units as shown to form a broken-dishes unit. Join the units in each row; press the seam allowances open. Join the rows; press. Each unit should measure 2½" square.

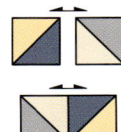 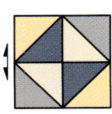

**3** Repeat steps 1 and 2 to make 20 units.

**4** Join four broken-dishes units to form a row; press the seam allowances open. Repeat to make a second row of four units and two rows of six units. The four-unit row should be 2½" x 8½". The six-unit row should be 2½" x 12½".

Make 2.

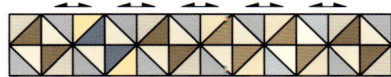

Make 2.

**5** Sew the four-unit rows to the sides of the quilt center; press the seam allowances away from the center. Sew the six-unit rows to the top and bottom; press. The piece should measure 12½" square.

## Assembling the Outer Border

**1** Draw a diagonal line from corner to corner on the wrong side of the 52 indigo 2½" squares and the four indigo 3" squares.

**2** Place a marked indigo 2½" square on one end of a cream rectangle with right sides together. Sew on the drawn line. Trim the seam allowances to ¼", and then press the indigo square away from the cream rectangle. The unit should measure 2½" x 3".

**3** Place a second marked indigo 2½" square on the opposite end of the unit, orienting the line in the same direction. Sew, trim, and press the unit as in step 2. Make 12 left-pointing units. Make 12 right-pointing units in the same manner, but press the seam allowances toward the cream fabric. The units should each be 2½" x 3".

Make 12 of each.

**4** Place a marked indigo 2½" square on one corner of a cream 3" square; sew on the line, trim, and press as before. Place a marked indigo 3" square on the opposite corner of the cream square, orienting the line in the same direction. Sew, trim, and press. Make four corner units. each should measure 3" square.

Make 4.

**5** Join six rectangle units in a row as shown; press the seam allowances in one direction. Make four border rows. Each row should be 3" x 12½".

Make 4.

**6** Sew a corner unit to each end of two of the border rows, aligning the cream diagonals. Press the seam allowances toward the rectangle units. Each row should be 3" x 17½".

Make 2.

**7** Sew the short border rows to the sides of the quilt center; press the seam allowances toward the outer border. Sew the long border rows to the top and bottom of the quilt center and press.

Quilt assembly

## Finishing the Quilt

Go to ShopMartingale.com/HowtoQuilt for more details on quilting and finishing.

**1** Layer the backing, batting, and quilt top; baste the layers together. Hand or machine quilt as desired. The quilt shown was machine quilted in the ditch and echo quilted around the flying geese and outer border diagonals to add definition.

**2** Use the brown-check 1⅛"-wide strips to make single-fold binding and attach it to the quilt.

### *Opposites are fun!*

Which describes your current status better:

☐ Streamlined Stash **OR** Supersized Stash ☑

☐ Press Seam Allowances Open **OR** Press to One Side ☑

☑ Salty **OR** Sweet ☐

☑ Steam **OR** No Steam ☐

☑ Prewashing **OR** No Prewashing ☐

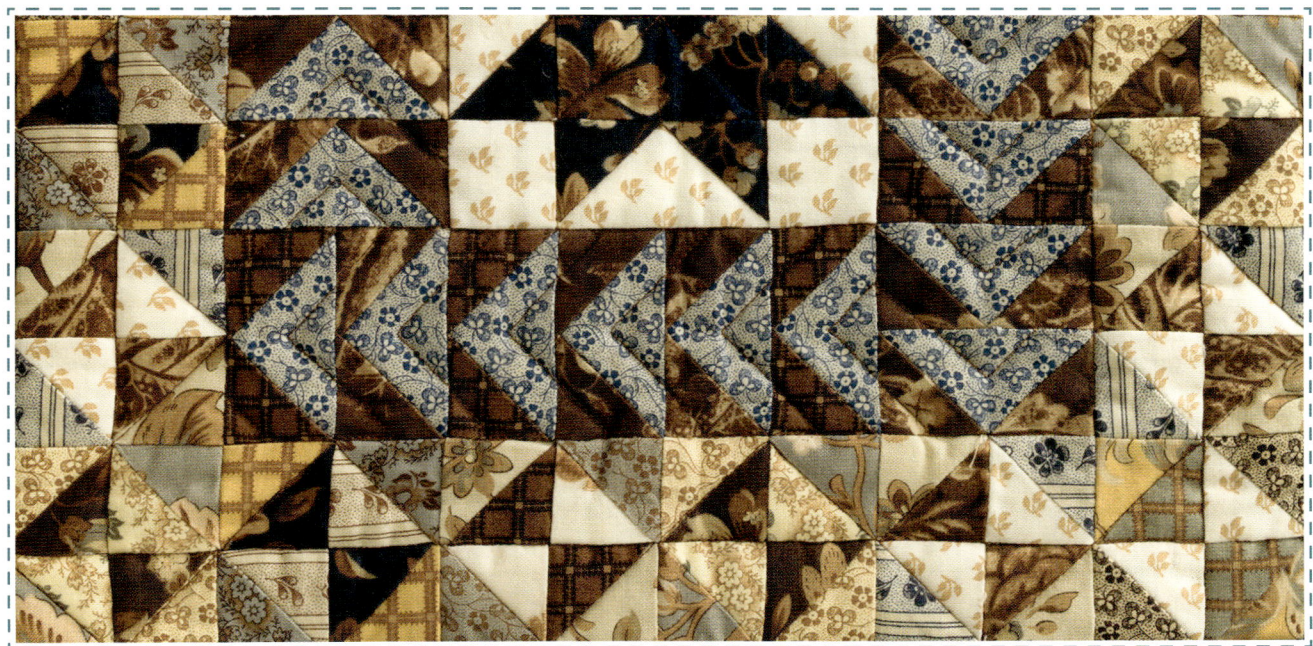

# Ideas for Your Mini-Quilt Gallery

Making mini-quilts is fun, but what do I do with them when I'm done? Maybe you've heard yourself muttering that phrase, or at least thinking to yourself, "How would I arrange them together?" Take heart. Here are a few ideas to help jump-start your creative process. We played with dimensions of actual mini-quilts in this book, but you can adapt these groupings for the mix you make. Friends will marvel at your clever collection of minis!

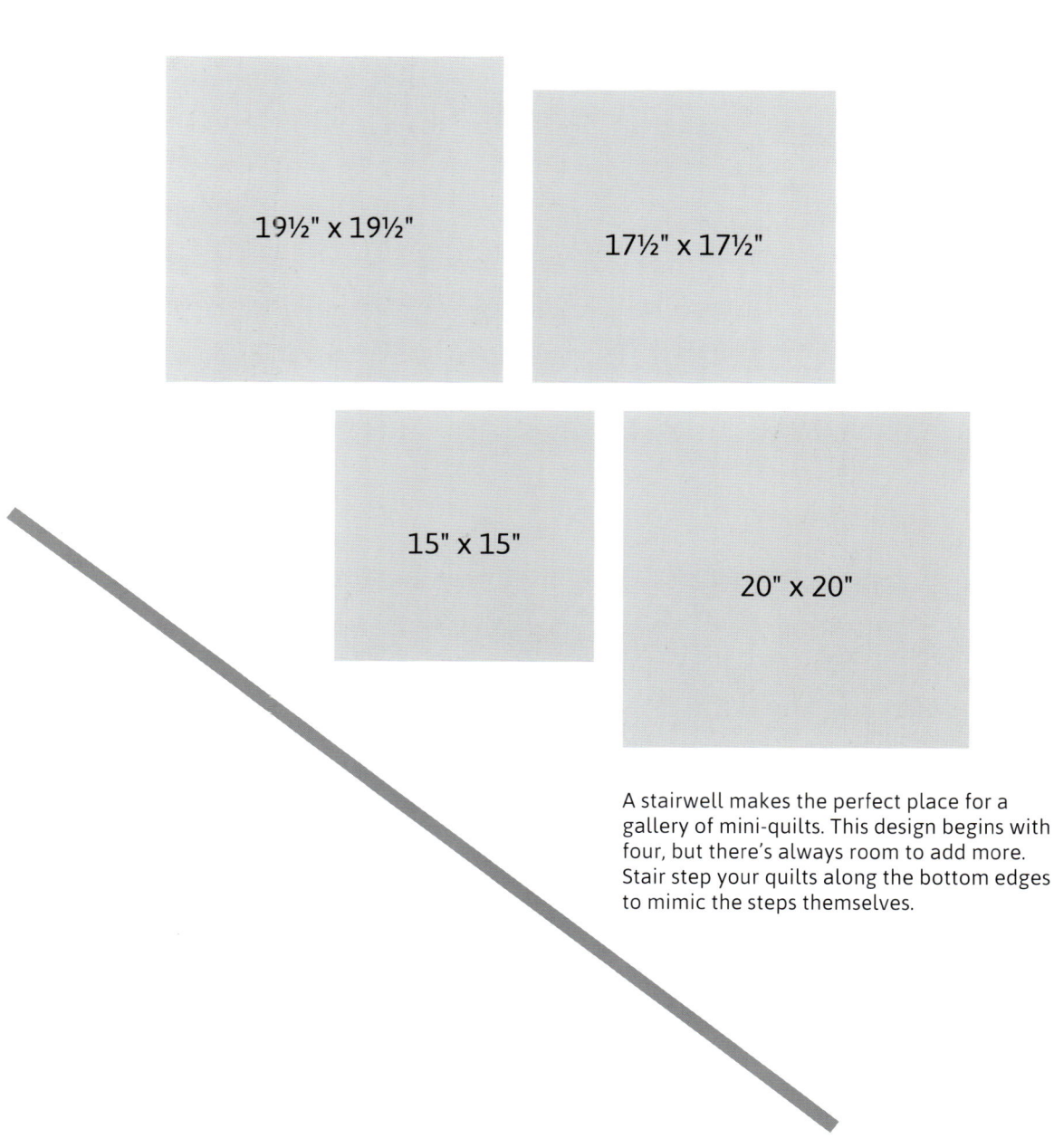

19½" x 19½"

17½" x 17½"

15" x 15"

20" x 20"

A stairwell makes the perfect place for a gallery of mini-quilts. This design begins with four, but there's always room to add more. Stair step your quilts along the bottom edges to mimic the steps themselves.

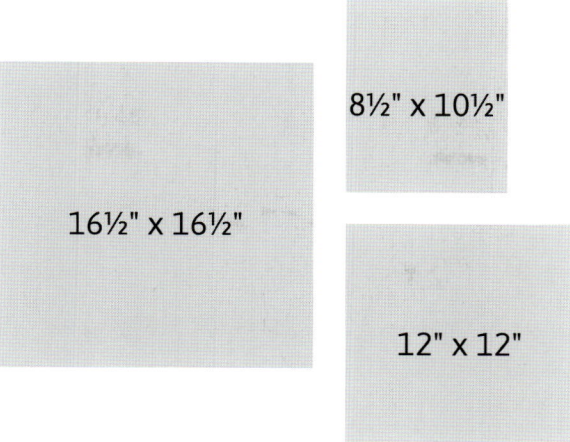

8½" x 10½"

16½" x 16½"

12" x 12"

One design rule of thumb is that anything is better in threes. So a trio of minis can work well above a sofa table or settee. Keep in mind that even with disparate sizes, you can create continuity by keeping the vertical and horizontal spaces between quilts equal.

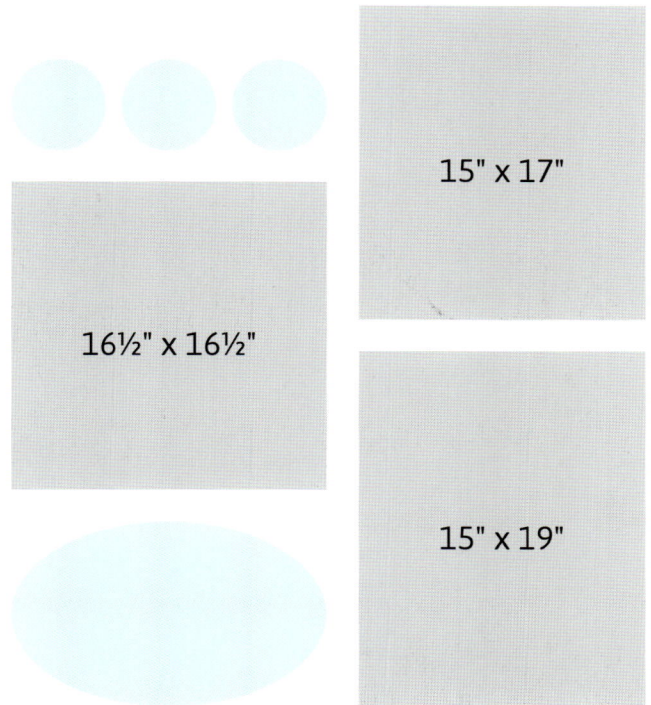

15" x 17"

16½" x 16½"

15" x 19"

Imagine filling this space as though it were a big rectangle on the wall. It doesn't have to be all quilts all the time. Think about adding other elements for texture and interest. Perhaps it's porthole picture frames or a treasured platter. Half the fun is in finding the objects to add to your mix!

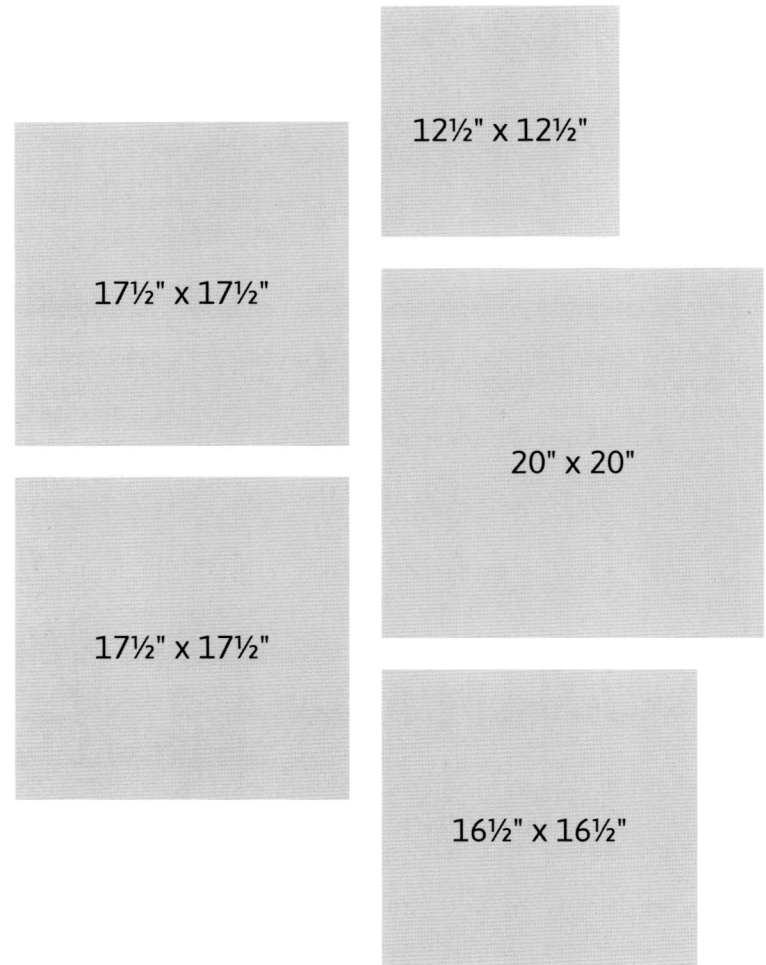

Arrangements that have organic shapes (those without regular borders or specific boundaries) often work best when you're grouping unlike-sized elements. Odd numbers of objects, as a rule, are more visually pleasing. So go for it—five quilts? seven quilts? maybe nine quilts? You be the judge.

# Mini Basics

*Here you'll find information on embroidery stitches and binding choices. If you'd like more detailed quiltmaking instructions, you'll find free, downloadable information on a variety of quilting topics at ShopMartingale.com/HowtoQuilt.*

## Embroidery Stitches

Several of the miniature quilts in this book have embroidered details or embellishments. Hand stitching adds an element of texture and charm that's well worth the effort.

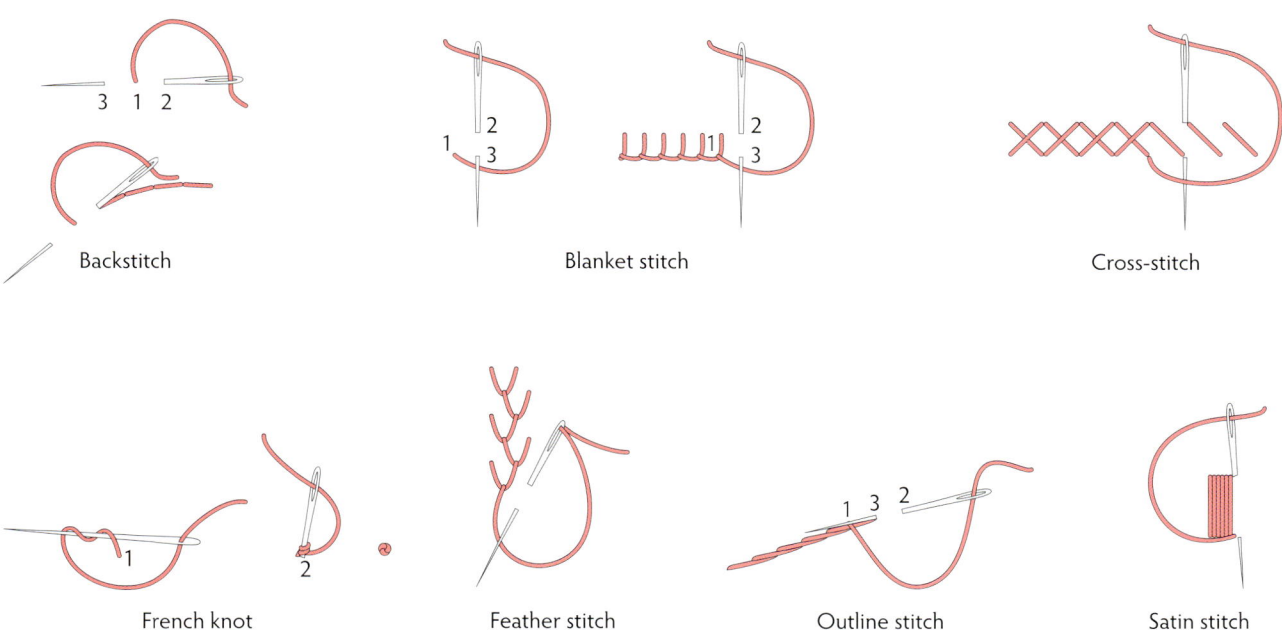

Backstitch

Blanket stitch

Cross-stitch

French knot

Feather stitch

Outline stitch

Satin stitch

## Binding Mini-Quilts

Each designer has provided the binding width used on the quilt shown. Preferences vary, with many quilters preferring a narrower binding on small quilts. Strips may be cut anywhere from 1⅛" wide for a single-fold binding to 2" to 2½" wide for a double-fold binding.

Betsy Chutchian, who designed and made Mini Medallion on page 70, likes a single-fold binding on small quilts because it makes for a flatter binding and looks like the bindings on antique quilts.

**Things to consider:**

**End use.** Will the quilt be heavily used for a table topper or a doll quilt? If so, a double-fold binding would be best for durability.

**Batting thickness.** If you use a thick batting, you may want to use wide binding strips to accommodate the thickness. Narrower, 2"-wide binding strips work best with thin, low-loft battings.

**Scale.** If you want your quilt to look somewhat like a miniature version of a larger quilt, then cut 2"-wide strips for a double-fold binding or 1⅛"-wide strips for single-fold binding.

# About the Contributors

### Lisa Bongean
A designer for Moda Fabrics, Lisa loves quilting, gardening, reading, and hunting for antiques. She and her husband Nick own Primitive Gatherings Quilt Shop and travel to quilting shows where Lisa teaches and shares her designs. You can find her at LisaBongean.com.

### Vanessa Christenson
The owner of V and Co., Vanessa designs and sews an array of bags, quilts, and accessories for the home. When not sewing or blogging, she enjoys reading, thrifting, decorating, organizing everything in sight, and spending time with her family. Visit VanessaChristenson.com.

### Betsy Chutchian
Betsy is an author, a designer for Moda Fabrics, and the cofounder of the 19th-Century Patchwork Divas. She developed a passionate interest in fabric, quilts, sewing, and history as a child. She began teaching quiltmaking in 1990 and enjoys sharing her passion for reproducing 19th-century quilts.

### Sandy Gervais
Sewing and art have always been a part of Sandy's life. She learned to sew at an early age. In 1992 she founded a quilt-pattern company, Pieces From My Heart, and her patterns were a hit. She was soon designing for Moda Fabrics. Visit her at PiecesFromMyHeart.net.

### Lynne Hagmeier
A passion for vintage quilts inspired Lynne to take her first quilting class in 1987. Working in a quilt shop and stitching small quilts led to selling patterns for the quilts she designed. Lynne has been designing fabric lines for Moda Fabrics for 15 years. Find her at KTQuilts.com.

### Brigitte Heitland
Brigitte is a textile and interior designer, the owner of Zen Chic, and a fabric designer for Moda Fabrics. She learned to sew while growing up in Germany. In 2010, Brigitte created her brand, Zen Chic. She debuted at the Spring Quilt Market 2011 trade show, where her booth won an award. Visit BHeitland.wix.com/zenchic.

### Jen Kingwell
A former midwife, Jen has always been fascinated by color and pattern. Her interest in quilting became an obsession and eventually grew into her second career. She owns Amitié Textiles, one of Australia's leading fabric and quilting stores, in Melbourne. Check out her blog at AmitieTextiles.blogspot.com.

### Sherri McConnell
Sherri received her first sewing machine when she was about 10 years old and has been sewing clothing and home-decor items ever since. After receiving a "gentle push" from her grandmother, she branched out into quilting and hasn't stopped. Visit AQuiltingLife.com.

### Me and My Sister Designs
Sisters Barbara Groves and Mary Jacobson make up the popular design team of Me and My Sister Designs. In addition to a line of quilt patterns, they have designed several fabric lines for Moda Fabrics. Visit MeAndMySisterDesigns.com.

### Carrie Nelson
Fans of Carrie Nelson may not know her by her given name, but they surely know her by her pattern-designer name, Miss Rosie. Carrie is now the guru of social media at Moda Fabrics, but occasionally she still slips into Miss Rosie mode to design yet another clever scrappy pattern.

### Camille Roskelley
Camille is a quilter and pattern designer. She is part of the mother-daughter team that designs the Bonnie and Camille fabric line for Moda Fabrics. Camille started her successful pattern company, Thimble Blossoms, in 2007. You can find her at ThimbleBlossoms.com.

### Laurie Simpson
Laurie is a lifelong needle artist whose quilts have been featured in publications such as *Country Home, Coastal Living, Architectural Digest, American Patchwork & Quilting, McCall's Quilting,* and *The Wool Street Journal.* Visit Laurie at MinickandSimpson.blogspot.com.

### Edyta Sitar
The owner of Laundry Basket Quilts, Edyta fell in love with fabric as a child. She expresses her passion by designing quilts in addition to fabrics for Moda Fabrics. Edyta travels and teaches quilters of all levels. Visit LaundryBasketQuilts.com.

### Pat Sloan
Pat is a quilt designer, author, teacher, radio/podcast show producer and host, and fabric designer. Her passion for making, sharing, and talking about quilts is limitless. Pat travels around the world teaching and hosts several Internet groups. Find her at PatSloan.com.

### Anne Sutton
Anne has always loved sewing and crafts, especially appliqué. For her, designing for Moda Fabrics is a dream come true. Her style ranges from sweet sophistication to whimsical. She enjoys spending her days in her Northern California loft studio. Visit Anne at BunnyHillDesigns.com.